From Zero to Hero in Everyday Life : Unleash your Potential, Transform your Reality

Benjamin Drath

Published by Benjamin Drath, 2023.

While every precaution has been taken in the preparation of this book, the publisher assumes no responsibility for errors or omissions, or for damages resulting from the use of the information contained herein.

FROM ZERO TO HERO IN EVERYDAY LIFE : UNLEASH YOUR POTENTIAL, TRANSFORM YOUR REALITY

First edition. July 3, 2023.

ISBN: 979-8223144380

Written by Benjamin Drath.

Table of Contents

Chapter 1: The significance of personal development.

———

P ersonal development is a lifelong journey of self-improvement and growth. In this chapter, we explore the profound significance of personal development in various aspects of our lives.

At its core, personal development involves the intentional pursuit of knowledge, skills, and experiences that contribute to our overall well-being and success. It encompasses both our personal and professional lives, helping us become better versions of ourselves.

One of the key aspects of personal development is self-awareness. Through introspection and reflection, we gain a deeper understanding of our values, strengths, weaknesses, and passions. This self-awareness provides a solid foundation for personal growth, allowing us to make informed decisions and take actions that align with our authentic selves.

Personal development plays a crucial role in enhancing our self-esteem and self-confidence. As we acquire new knowledge and skills, achieve personal milestones, and overcome challenges, we build a strong belief in our abilities and worth. This confidence empowers us to pursue our goals with determination and resilience.

Moreover, personal development fosters a positive mindset. It helps us shift our perspective from a fixed mindset, where we believe our abilities are static, to a growth mindset, where we see challenges as opportunities for learning and growth. By embracing a growth mindset, we open ourselves up to new possibilities and continuously strive for improvement.

In today's rapidly changing world, personal development is essential for adaptability and success. The skills and knowledge we acquire through personal growth enable us to stay ahead in our careers, navigate challenges, and seize opportunities. As we enhance our skill set and broaden our knowledge base, we become more valuable assets in our professional lives.

Personal development also plays a significant role in our relationships and interactions with others. It enhances our communication skills, empathy, and emotional intelligence, allowing us to forge deeper connections and understand different perspectives. By investing in personal development, we become better equipped to navigate conflicts, build healthy relationships, and collaborate effectively.

Beyond individual benefits, personal development contributes to the betterment of society as a whole. When individuals strive for personal growth, they become more compassionate, empathetic, and socially conscious. They actively seek opportunities to contribute to their communities and make a positive impact in the world. Personal development, therefore, has the potential to create a ripple effect of positive change.

It's important to note that personal development is not a one-size-fits-all approach. Each individual's journey is unique, and personal development should be tailored to individual strengths, values, and aspirations. What works for one person may not work for another. It's essential to explore various methods, such as reading books, attending seminars, seeking mentors, or engaging in reflective practices, to find what resonates with us personally.

In conclusion, personal development is of immense significance in our lives. It empowers us to uncover our true potential, develop a positive mindset, and cultivate skills and knowledge that contribute to our personal and professional success. By embarking on a journey of personal growth, we become the architects of our own lives, constantly evolving and striving for a better version of ourselves.

Chapter 2: Embracing a growth mindset.

———

I n this chapter, we delve into the concept of a growth mindset and its profound impact on personal development and achievement. We explore the power of adopting a growth mindset and provide strategies to cultivate this mindset in our lives.

A growth mindset is the belief that our abilities, intelligence, and talents can be developed and improved through dedication, effort, and a willingness to learn. It is the opposite of a fixed mindset, which assumes that our qualities and capabilities are predetermined and unchangeable.

Embracing a growth mindset opens up a world of possibilities. It allows us to view challenges as opportunities for growth and learning, rather than as insurmountable obstacles. When faced with setbacks or failures, individuals with a growth mindset see them as temporary setbacks and valuable learning experiences, rather than indications of their innate limitations.

One of the key aspects of cultivating a growth mindset is embracing the power of yet. By adding the word "yet" to our statements, such as "I haven't mastered this skill yet," we acknowledge that growth and improvement are ongoing processes. This simple shift in language helps us develop a belief in our ability to learn and grow over time.

Another strategy to foster a growth mindset is reframing failure. Rather than viewing failure as a personal reflection of our abilities, we can see it as an essential step on the path to success. Failure provides valuable feedback and insights that guide our future efforts and allow us to make necessary adjustments.

Effort and perseverance are integral components of a growth mindset. Individuals with a growth mindset understand that progress and mastery require sustained effort and a willingness to embrace challenges. They see effort as a necessary and valuable part of the learning process, rather than as a sign of weakness or incompetence.

Cultivating a growth mindset also involves seeking out feedback and embracing constructive criticism. Feedback provides us with valuable insights into areas where we can improve and grow. By welcoming feedback and seeing it as an opportunity for growth, we can accelerate our development and overcome potential blind spots.

In addition to these strategies, it is important to surround ourselves with individuals who embody a growth mindset. By interacting with people who embrace challenges, persist in the face of setbacks, and celebrate the success of others, we create a supportive environment that reinforces our own growth mindset.

Practicing mindfulness and self-reflection can also contribute to the cultivation of a growth mindset. By paying attention to our thoughts and beliefs, we can identify and challenge any fixed mindset tendencies. Engaging in regular self-reflection allows us to examine our mindset and make intentional shifts towards a growth-oriented perspective.

It's important to acknowledge that developing a growth mindset is a continuous process that requires effort and commitment. It may not happen overnight, and setbacks or moments of self-doubt are natural. However, with practice and perseverance, we can gradually shift our mindset and experience the transformative power of a growth-oriented perspective.

Embracing a growth mindset has far-reaching implications beyond personal development. It impacts our relationships, careers, and overall well-being. It enables us to approach challenges with resilience and optimism, to pursue our goals with passion and determination, and to continuously evolve and grow as individuals.

In conclusion, adopting a growth mindset is a powerful tool for personal growth and achievement. By recognizing that our abilities and intelligence can be developed, we open ourselves up to a world of possibilities. Through strategies such as reframing failure, embracing effort, seeking feedback, and surrounding ourselves with growth-minded individuals, we can cultivate a mindset that fosters continuous learning and growth. By embracing a growth mindset, we empower ourselves to overcome challenges, unleash our potential, and create a fulfilling and successful life.

Chapter 3: Overcoming limiting beliefs.

―――

In this chapter, we explore the concept of limiting beliefs and provide strategies to overcome them. Limiting beliefs are deeply ingrained negative thoughts or perceptions about ourselves and our capabilities that hinder our personal growth and success.

Limiting beliefs can stem from various sources, such as past experiences, societal conditioning, or negative self-talk. They often manifest as self-defeating thoughts such as "I'm not smart enough," "I don't deserve success," or "I will never be able to achieve my goals." These beliefs create self-imposed barriers that prevent us from reaching our full potential.

The first step in overcoming limiting beliefs is to identify and acknowledge them. It requires self-awareness and a willingness to examine our thoughts and beliefs objectively. We can start by paying attention to our self-talk and noticing recurring negative patterns or thoughts that hold us back.

Once we have identified our limiting beliefs, we can challenge their validity. We can ask ourselves questions such as, "What evidence do I have to support this belief?" or "Is this belief serving me or holding me back?" This process of critical examination helps us gain perspective and realize that our limiting beliefs are often based on assumptions or past experiences that may no longer be relevant.

An effective strategy for overcoming limiting beliefs is to reframe them. We can replace negative self-talk with positive affirmations and empowering statements. For example, if we believe, "I'm not good enough," we can reframe it as "I am constantly growing and improving."

By consciously shifting our internal dialogue, we can reprogram your subconscious mind and create new empowering beliefs.

Another approach is to seek evidence that contradicts our limiting beliefs. We can look for examples of people who have overcome similar challenges or achieved what we aspire to achieve. By surrounding ourselves with positive role models and success stories, we expand our belief in what is possible for ourselves.

Taking action is crucial in overcoming limiting beliefs. By stepping outside our comfort zones and confronting our fears, we gradually build evidence that challenges our self-imposed limitations. Each small step forward reinforces our belief in our capabilities and breaks down the barriers created by limiting beliefs.

Support systems and accountability partners play a vital role in overcoming limiting beliefs. By sharing our goals and aspirations with trusted friends, family members, or mentors, we invite their support and encouragement. They can provide valuable perspective, challenge our limiting beliefs, and hold us accountable for taking action towards our goals.

Mindfulness practices can also help in overcoming limiting beliefs. By observing our thoughts and emotions without judgment, we create space to challenge and reframe our negative beliefs. Mindfulness allows us to detach from our limiting beliefs and cultivate a more compassionate and empowering mindset.

It's important to recognize that overcoming limiting beliefs is an ongoing process that requires patience and persistence. It's not a one-time event but a continuous journey of self-discovery and personal growth. Setbacks and moments of doubt are normal, but with determination and a commitment to self-improvement, we can gradually chip away at our limiting beliefs and create new empowering narratives.

By overcoming limiting beliefs, we open ourselves up to new possibilities and unleash our full potential. We free ourselves from self-imposed limitations and create a mindset that embraces growth, resilience, and success. With each limiting belief we overcome, we move closer to living a more authentic, fulfilling, and extraordinary life.

In conclusion, overcoming limiting beliefs is essential for personal growth and success. By identifying, challenging, and reframing our negative beliefs, we can break free from self-imposed barriers and create new empowering narratives. With a mindset rooted in possibility and self-belief, we can achieve remarkable things and create a life that aligns with our true potential.

Chapter 4: Setting and pursuing goals.

———

In this chapter, we delve into the process of setting and pursuing goals, which is essential for personal growth and achievement. Goals provide direction, motivation, and a sense of purpose in our lives. We explore effective strategies for setting goals and provide practical tips for pursuing them.

Setting goals begins with defining a clear vision of what we want to achieve. By envisioning our desired outcome, we create a roadmap that guides our actions and decisions. It's important to set goals that are meaningful and aligned with our values, passions, and aspirations. When our goals are in sync with our authentic selves, we are more likely to stay motivated and committed to their pursuit.

To make our goals more actionable and measurable, it's helpful to follow the SMART framework. SMART stands for Specific, Measurable, Achievable, Relevant, and Time-bound. Specific goals provide clarity on what exactly we want to achieve, while measurable goals allow us to track our progress and celebrate milestones. Achievable goals are realistic and within our reach, while relevant goals align with our broader aspirations and values. Finally, time-bound goals have a deadline or timeline, which adds a sense of urgency and accountability.

Breaking down goals into smaller, manageable steps is crucial for progress and momentum. By chunking down our goals into actionable tasks, we avoid overwhelm and gain a clear roadmap for implementation. Each small step taken towards our goals builds confidence and propels us forward.

It's important to stay flexible and adaptable in the pursuit of our goals. Sometimes unexpected obstacles or opportunities arise, requiring us to adjust our plans. By maintaining a growth mindset and being open to change, we can navigate these challenges and make necessary adjustments to stay on track.

Accountability plays a significant role in goal pursuit. Sharing our goals with trusted individuals, such as friends, family, or mentors, can provide support, encouragement, and an external source of accountability. Regular check-ins, progress updates, and feedback from our accountability partners can help us stay focused and motivated.

Visualizing our goals and creating a compelling vision board can also enhance goal attainment. By creating a visual representation of our goals, we engage our subconscious mind and reinforce our commitment. Regularly visualizing our goals and connecting with the emotions associated with their achievement helps to strengthen our motivation and belief in their attainability.

In the pursuit of our goals, it's crucial to celebrate milestones and acknowledge progress along the way. Recognizing and celebrating our achievements not only boosts our confidence and motivation but also provides a sense of fulfillment and satisfaction. Celebrating small wins creates positive reinforcement and propels us forward with renewed energy.

Additionally, it's important to cultivate a growth-oriented mindset throughout the goal-setting process. Embracing a mindset that sees setbacks as learning opportunities and failures as stepping stones to success allows us to stay resilient and persistent. By reframing challenges as valuable experiences, we maintain a positive outlook and are more likely to persevere.

Regularly reviewing and reassessing our goals is also vital. As we grow and evolve, our aspirations may change. Periodically evaluating our goals ensures that they remain relevant and aligned with our current values and passions. It's okay to modify or replace goals if they no longer resonate with our authentic selves.

In conclusion, setting and pursuing goals is a fundamental aspect of personal growth and achievement. By setting specific, measurable, achievable, relevant, and time-bound goals, breaking them down into actionable steps, staying accountable, and maintaining a growth mindset, we can make remarkable progress in our lives. With determination, resilience, and a clear vision, we can turn our dreams into reality and experience the satisfaction of personal fulfillment.

Chapter 5: The power of positive habits.

In this chapter, we explore the transformative power of positive habits and their impact on personal development and success. Habits are the small actions and behaviors that we engage in repeatedly, often unconsciously. They shape our daily routines and have a profound influence on our overall well-being and productivity.

Positive habits are behaviors that contribute to our growth, well-being, and success. They are the building blocks of personal development, allowing us to make progress towards our goals and cultivate a fulfilling and meaningful life. In this chapter, we will discuss strategies for developing and maintaining positive habits.

The first step in cultivating positive habits is self-awareness. We need to identify the habits that currently exist in our lives and evaluate their impact. By observing our daily routines and reflecting on how certain habits align with our goals and values, we can determine which habits are serving us well and which ones may be hindering our progress.

To develop positive habits, it's important to start small and be consistent. By focusing on one habit at a time, we can direct our energy and attention towards creating lasting change. Breaking down larger habits into smaller, manageable actions makes them more attainable and increases our chances of success. Consistency is key, as it allows the habit to become ingrained and automatic over time.

Creating a supportive environment is crucial for the development of positive habits. Our environment greatly influences our behaviors and choices. By surrounding ourselves with cues and reminders that reinforce our desired habits, we increase the likelihood of sticking to them. For example, if our goal is to exercise regularly, we can place our workout clothes and equipment in a visible and accessible location, making it easier to engage in physical activity.

Another effective strategy is to utilize habit stacking or habit chaining. This involves attaching a new habit to an existing one, creating a sequence of actions that reinforce each other. For instance, if our goal is to read more books, we can establish a habit of reading for 15 minutes after brushing our teeth before bed. By linking the new habit to an existing one, we increase the chances of it becoming ingrained in our routine.

Accountability and tracking our progress are essential for maintaining positive habits. By sharing our goals and habits with others, we invite their support and create a sense of external accountability. Regularly tracking our progress, either through journaling, habit-tracking apps, or other methods, helps us stay motivated and celebrate our achievements. It also allows us to identify any patterns or challenges that may be hindering our habit formation.

The power of positive reinforcement should not be underestimated. Celebrating our successes and rewarding ourselves for sticking to our desired habits creates a positive feedback loop. This reinforces the behavior and makes it more likely to be repeated. Rewards can be simple, such as treating ourselves to a favorite activity or indulging in a small pleasure, but they play a significant role in strengthening the habit.

Over time, positive habits become ingrained and part of our identity. They require less effort and willpower to maintain. This is known as habit stacking or the compound effect. As we continue to develop and maintain positive habits, they create a ripple effect that positively impacts other areas of our lives. For example, cultivating a habit of daily meditation may not only improve our mental well-being but also enhance our focus, productivity, and relationships.

It's important to note that breaking negative or unhealthy habits can be challenging. It requires self-discipline, perseverance, and a commitment to change. However, by replacing negative habits with positive ones and consciously choosing behaviors that align with our values and goals, we can gradually transform our lives.

In conclusion, positive habits have the power to shape our lives and contribute to our personal development and success. By cultivating self-awareness, starting small, creating a supportive environment, utilizing habit stacking, maintaining accountability, tracking progress, and reinforcing positive behavior, we can establish a foundation for long-lasting positive habits.

Developing positive habits is a continuous process that requires effort and commitment. It's important to be patient with ourselves and understand that change takes time. Some days may be more challenging than others, but by staying focused on our goals and maintaining a positive mindset, we can overcome obstacles and persevere.

Positive habits not only benefit us individually but also have a ripple effect on other areas of our lives. For example, establishing a habit of regular exercise not only improves our physical health but also boosts our energy levels, enhances our mood, and increases our productivity in other areas of life. Similarly, cultivating a habit of practicing gratitude can positively impact our relationships, mental well-being, and overall outlook on life.

It's important to regularly reassess our habits and make adjustments as needed. As we grow and evolve, our priorities and goals may change. By regularly evaluating our habits and their alignment with our current aspirations, we ensure that they continue to serve us well and contribute to our personal growth.

In summary, positive habits have the power to shape our lives and propel us towards personal development and success. By cultivating self-awareness, starting small, creating a supportive environment, maintaining accountability, tracking progress, and reinforcing positive behavior, we can establish a solid foundation for lasting positive habits. With time, dedication, and perseverance, these habits become second nature, transforming our lives in remarkable ways. Embracing positive habits allows us to live more fulfilling, productive, and meaningful lives.

Chapter 6: Developing mental resilience.

———

In this chapter, we delve into the concept of mental resilience and its significance in navigating life's challenges and setbacks. Mental resilience refers to our ability to adapt, bounce back, and maintain a positive mindset in the face of adversity. It is a crucial skill for personal growth, success, and overall well-being.

Life is full of ups and downs, and developing mental resilience allows us to navigate through the inevitable challenges with grace and strength. Resilience is not about avoiding difficulties or denying negative emotions; rather, it is about acknowledging them, learning from them, and using them as opportunities for growth.

The first step in developing mental resilience is cultivating a positive and optimistic mindset. Optimism doesn't mean ignoring the reality of difficult situations; rather, it is the belief that we have the strength and capability to overcome them. By adopting a positive outlook and reframing challenges as opportunities for learning and growth, we can maintain resilience in the face of adversity.

Another important aspect of mental resilience is self-care. Taking care of our physical, emotional, and mental well-being provides us with the necessary resources to cope with stress and bounce back from setbacks. Prioritizing activities that recharge and rejuvenate us, such as exercise, meditation, spending time in nature, or engaging in hobbies, helps to build resilience and maintain a balanced perspective.

Building a support network is crucial for developing mental resilience. Surrounding ourselves with positive and supportive individuals who believe in our potential and provide encouragement during challenging times can significantly impact our ability to bounce back. Seeking guidance, advice, and emotional support from trusted friends, family members, or mentors can provide valuable perspective and help us build resilience.

Developing emotional intelligence is also important in building mental resilience. Emotional intelligence involves recognizing and understanding our own emotions, as well as empathizing with others. By developing this skill, we can effectively manage our emotions, regulate stress, and navigate interpersonal relationships more effectively. Emotional intelligence helps us stay centered and resilient in the face of adversity.

Practicing mindfulness and self-reflection is a powerful tool for developing mental resilience. Mindfulness involves being fully present in the current moment, observing our thoughts and emotions without judgment. It allows us to cultivate a greater sense of self-awareness, manage stress more effectively, and make better decisions. Self-reflection enables us to learn from our experiences, identify patterns, and develop strategies for coping with future challenges.

Building problem-solving skills is essential in developing mental resilience. Instead of becoming overwhelmed by problems, resilient individuals approach them as opportunities for growth and find creative solutions. Developing problem-solving skills involves breaking down challenges into manageable steps, seeking alternative perspectives, and being open to new ideas and approaches.

An important aspect of mental resilience is embracing failure as a stepping stone to success. Resilient individuals understand that failure is a natural part of the learning process and an opportunity for growth. They view setbacks as temporary and see them as opportunities to learn, adapt, and improve. By reframing failure as feedback and using it to refine our strategies, we build resilience and increase our chances of future success.

Finally, maintaining a sense of purpose and meaning in life is crucial for developing mental resilience. When we have a clear sense of our values, goals, and what truly matters to us, we are better able to navigate through challenges and setbacks. A sense of purpose provides us with the motivation and resilience to persevere, even in the face of adversity.

In conclusion, developing mental resilience is essential for navigating life's challenges, bouncing back from setbacks, and achieving personal growth and success. By cultivating a positive mindset, practicing self-care, building a support network, developing emotional intelligence, practicing mindfulness, building problem-solving skills, embracing failure, and maintaining a sense of purpose, we can enhance our mental resilience. With resilience as our ally, we become better equipped to face adversity, overcome obstacles, and thrive in the face of challenges.

Mental resilience is not something that is innate or fixed. It is a skill that can be developed and strengthened over time. Like a muscle, the more we exercise and practice resilience, the stronger it becomes. It is important to remember that building mental resilience is a journey, and it requires effort and perseverance.

One effective strategy for developing mental resilience is to embrace a growth mindset. A growth mindset is the belief that our abilities and intelligence can be developed through dedication and hard work. By adopting this mindset, we see setbacks and failures as opportunities for growth and learning, rather than as indicators of our limitations. Cultivating a growth mindset allows us to bounce back from failures and setbacks with renewed determination and a focus on learning and improvement.

Building resilience also involves managing stress and developing effective coping mechanisms. Stress is an inevitable part of life, but how we respond to it can greatly impact our resilience. Engaging in stress-reducing activities such as exercise, meditation, deep breathing exercises, or engaging in hobbies can help us relax and recharge. Developing healthy coping mechanisms, such as seeking support from loved ones, journaling, or practicing mindfulness, can also help us navigate through stressful situations with resilience.

Another important aspect of developing mental resilience is building self-confidence and self-belief. Believing in our abilities and strengths gives us the courage to face challenges head-on and persevere in the face of adversity. Developing self-confidence involves recognizing and celebrating our achievements, embracing our unique qualities, and challenging self-limiting beliefs. By nurturing a positive self-image and cultivating self-compassion, we strengthen our mental resilience.

Building resilience also requires us to develop effective problem-solving and decision-making skills. When faced with challenges, resilient individuals are able to assess the situation, identify potential solutions, and take decisive action. Developing problem-solving skills involves breaking down complex problems into smaller, more manageable tasks, seeking input from others, and being open to alternative perspectives. Effective decision-making skills help us navigate through difficult choices with confidence and clarity.

Resilient individuals also practice self-care and prioritize their well-being. Taking care of our physical, emotional, and mental health is essential for building resilience. Getting enough restful sleep, maintaining a balanced diet, engaging in regular exercise, and nurturing healthy relationships all contribute to our overall well-being and strengthen our resilience. By taking care of ourselves, we build the foundation for resilience and the ability to face challenges with strength and determination.

Finally, developing a support network is crucial for building mental resilience. Surrounding ourselves with supportive and positive individuals who believe in our potential and provide encouragement during difficult times can make a significant difference. Sharing our experiences, seeking guidance, and receiving support from others can help us gain perspective, find solutions, and stay resilient in the face of adversity.

In conclusion, developing mental resilience is a vital skill for navigating life's challenges and setbacks. By embracing a growth mindset, managing stress, building self-confidence, developing problem-solving skills, practicing self-care, and building a support network, we can strengthen our mental resilience and thrive in the face of adversity. With resilience as our ally, we can face life's challenges head-on, grow from them, and create a fulfilling and successful life.

Chapter 7: Managing negative thoughts and emotions.

———

In this chapter, we explore the importance of managing negative thoughts and emotions and how it contributes to our overall well-being and personal growth. Our thoughts and emotions have a significant impact on our mental and emotional state, as well as our behavior and actions. Learning to effectively manage negative thoughts and emotions is essential for maintaining a positive mindset, improving relationships, and achieving success.

Negative thoughts can be self-defeating and limit our potential. They often stem from self-doubt, fear, or past experiences. These thoughts can lead to a downward spiral of negativity and hinder our ability to see opportunities or solutions. By recognizing and managing negative thoughts, we can regain control of our mindset and improve our overall outlook on life.

One effective strategy for managing negative thoughts is practicing mindfulness. Mindfulness involves being fully present in the moment and observing our thoughts without judgment. By becoming aware of our negative thoughts and acknowledging them, we can detach ourselves from them and prevent them from consuming our mind. Mindfulness allows us to create distance from negative thoughts and cultivate a more objective and balanced perspective.

Challenging and reframing negative thoughts is another powerful technique. Often, negative thoughts are based on distortions or irrational beliefs. By questioning the validity and accuracy of these thoughts, we can challenge their credibility. For example, if we find ourselves thinking, "I always fail at everything," we can challenge this thought by looking for evidence of times when we have succeeded or by reframing the situation as a learning opportunity rather than a failure. This process of cognitive restructuring helps to shift our perspective and replace negative thoughts with more positive and empowering ones.

Practicing self-compassion is vital in managing negative thoughts and emotions. Self-compassion involves treating ourselves with kindness, understanding, and acceptance, especially during difficult times. Instead of being self-critical or judgmental, we can offer ourselves support and empathy. Recognizing that everyone experiences negative thoughts and emotions at times allows us to be more compassionate towards ourselves and cultivate a healthier relationship with our inner dialogue.

Another effective strategy is engaging in activities that uplift our mood and shift our focus away from negative thoughts. This could include participating in hobbies, spending time with loved ones, engaging in physical exercise, or practicing relaxation techniques. These activities help to redirect our attention and generate positive emotions, thereby reducing the intensity of negative thoughts and emotions.

It is also important to develop healthy emotional regulation skills. Emotions are a natural part of being human, and it is crucial to acknowledge and process them effectively. Techniques such as deep breathing exercises, journaling, or talking to a trusted friend or therapist can help in understanding and managing emotions in a healthy way. By allowing ourselves to experience and express our emotions in a constructive manner, we can prevent them becoming overwhelming or controlling our actions.

Building emotional resilience is another aspect of managing negative thoughts and emotions. Emotional resilience is the ability to adapt and bounce back from adversity. It involves developing a strong support system, cultivating optimism, practicing self-care, and engaging in activities that enhance emotional well-being. Building emotional resilience allows us to navigate through challenging situations with greater ease and maintain a positive mindset.

Developing effective problem-solving skills is also important in managing negative thoughts and emotions. Often, negative thoughts arise when we feel stuck or unable to find a solution to a problem. By developing problem-solving skills, we can approach challenges more effectively, find solutions, and reduce the impact of negative thoughts. This involves breaking down problems into smaller, manageable steps, seeking support or advice, and being open to alternative solutions.

In conclusion, managing negative thoughts and emotions is essential for our well-being and personal growth. By practicing mindfulness, challenging negative thoughts, practicing self-compassion, engaging in mood-enhancing activities, developing emotional regulation skills, building emotional resilience, and developing problem-solving skills, we can effectively manage negative thoughts and emotions. By implementing these strategies, we can cultivate a more positive and empowered mindset, improve our relationships, and enhance our overall well-being.

It's important to remember that managing negative thoughts and emotions is an ongoing process. It requires self-awareness, patience, and practice. We may encounter setbacks or moments when negative thoughts seem overwhelming, but with persistence and the right tools, we can navigate through them.

It's helpful to create a support system of trusted individuals who can provide guidance and encouragement during challenging times. Sharing our experiences and seeking support not only helps us gain perspective but also reminds us that we are not alone in our struggles.

In addition to external support, self-reflection plays a crucial role in managing negative thoughts and emotions. Taking the time to understand the underlying causes of our negative thoughts and emotions can help us identify patterns and triggers. Through self-reflection, we can develop a deeper understanding of ourselves and work towards addressing the root causes of negativity.

Practicing self-care is also essential in managing negative thoughts and emotions. Taking care of our physical, emotional, and mental well-being creates a solid foundation for maintaining a positive mindset. Engaging in activities that bring us joy and relaxation, prioritizing restful sleep, nourishing our bodies with nutritious food, and engaging in regular exercise all contribute to our overall well-being and help us manage negative thoughts and emotions more effectively.

Developing a toolbox of coping mechanisms is valuable in managing negative thoughts and emotions. Different techniques work for different individuals, so it's important to explore and find what resonates with us personally. Some people find solace in activities such as meditation, deep breathing exercises, or journaling, while others find comfort in engaging in creative outlets or spending time in nature. Experimenting with different techniques allows us to discover what helps us process and manage negative thoughts and emotions in a healthy way.

Lastly, practicing gratitude can significantly impact our mindset and help manage negative thoughts and emotions. Focusing on what we are grateful for shifts our perspective from negativity to positivity. Incorporating a gratitude practice into our daily routine, such as writing down three things we are grateful for each day, can bring a sense of appreciation and contentment, reducing the power of negative thoughts.

In conclusion, managing negative thoughts and emotions is an important aspect of personal growth and well-being. By practicing mindfulness, challenging negative thoughts, cultivating self-compassion, engaging in mood-enhancing activities, developing emotional resilience, reflecting on our experiences, practicing self-care, and incorporating gratitude into our lives, we can effectively manage negative thoughts and emotions. Remember, it is a journey that requires patience and self-compassion, but with commitment and practice, we can cultivate a positive mindset and live a more fulfilling and balanced life.

Chapter 8: The art of self-reflection.

———

I n this chapter, we explore the importance of self-reflection as a powerful tool for personal growth, self-awareness, and achieving a fulfilling life. Self-reflection is the practice of looking inward, examining our thoughts, emotions, actions, and experiences to gain a deeper understanding of ourselves.

Self-reflection allows us to pause amidst the busyness of life and create space for introspection. It is a time for self-examination, where we can ask ourselves important questions and gain valuable insights. By engaging in self-reflection, we become more conscious of our beliefs, values, strengths, weaknesses, and patterns of behavior.

One of the key benefits of self-reflection is gaining self-awareness. When we take the time to reflect on our thoughts, feelings, and behaviors, we develop a clearer understanding of who we are as individuals. We become aware of our strengths and areas for improvement, as well as the impact we have on others and the world around us. Self-awareness is a fundamental aspect of personal growth, as it allows us to make conscious choices and align our actions with our values.

Self-reflection also helps us uncover the underlying motivations and triggers behind our thoughts and actions. It allows us to explore the root causes of our emotions and behaviors, which can be instrumental in breaking free from unhealthy patterns or limiting beliefs. By understanding the why behind our actions, we can make intentional changes and cultivate healthier habits and attitudes.

Through self-reflection, we gain clarity about our goals and aspirations. Taking the time to reflect on our desires, dreams, and passions helps us identify what truly matters to us. It allows us to set meaningful goals and align our actions with our aspirations. Self-reflection acts as a compass, guiding us towards a more purposeful and fulfilling life.

Another important aspect of self-reflection is learning from our experiences. By reflecting on past successes and failures, we can extract valuable lessons that inform our future decisions and actions. Self-reflection allows us to celebrate our achievements and acknowledge the progress we have made. It also helps us identify areas where we can improve and develop strategies for growth. Through this process, we cultivate a growth mindset and embrace a continuous learning mentality.

Practicing self-reflection also promotes emotional well-being. By acknowledging and processing our emotions, we can better understand and manage them. Self-reflection provides an opportunity to express and release pent-up emotions, reducing stress and promoting a sense of inner peace. It enables us to cultivate self-compassion and develop a kinder relationship with ourselves.

There are various techniques to engage in self-reflection. Journaling is a popular method, where we can write down our thoughts, feelings, and observations. This process allows us to externalize our inner world and gain new insights through the act of writing. Meditation and mindfulness practices also facilitate self-reflection by quieting the mind and creating a space for self-awareness. Taking regular breaks for solitude and introspection, away from distractions, provides an opportunity to reflect deeply.

While self-reflection can be a solitary practice, it is also beneficial to seek external perspectives and feedback. Engaging in meaningful conversations with trusted friends, mentors, or therapists can offer valuable insights and alternative viewpoints. Others may notice patterns or strengths that we might have overlooked, providing us with new perspectives and opportunities for growth.

Incorporating self-reflection into our daily lives requires intention and commitment. Designating dedicated time for self-reflection, whether it's a few minutes each day or a longer period on a weekly basis, helps make it a consistent practice. Creating a supportive environment that encourages self-reflection, such as a quiet space or a journaling routine, can further enhance the experience.

In conclusion, the art of self-reflection is a powerful tool for personal growth and self-awareness. By engaging in self-reflection, we gain valuable insights into ourselves, our beliefs, values, strengths, weaknesses, and patterns of behavior. It allows us to develop self-awareness, understand our motivations and triggers, gain clarity about our goals, learn from our experiences, and promote emotional well-being.

Self-reflection is a practice that can be incorporated into our daily lives in various ways. Journaling, meditation, mindfulness, and meaningful conversations with others are effective methods to engage in self-reflection. It requires carving out dedicated time, creating a supportive environment, and committing to the process.

When practicing self-reflection, it is important to approach it with openness, curiosity, and non-judgment. It is not about criticizing ourselves or dwelling on past mistakes but rather about gaining insights and using them as stepping stones for growth. Self-compassion plays a crucial role in self-reflection, as it allows us to be kind and understanding towards ourselves during the process.

Self-reflection helps us develop a deeper understanding of ourselves, enabling us to make conscious choices aligned with our values and aspirations. It acts as a compass, guiding us towards a more purposeful and fulfilling life. It also promotes continuous learning, as we reflect on our experiences, extract lessons, and apply them to future situations.

By engaging in self-reflection, we can identify and challenge limiting beliefs, cultivate a growth mindset, and develop strategies for personal development. It allows us to celebrate our successes, acknowledge our progress, and set meaningful goals for the future. Self-reflection supports emotional well-being by providing an opportunity to process and manage our emotions, fostering self-compassion, and reducing stress.

Self-reflection is a lifelong practice. As we grow and evolve, our reflections will deepen and evolve as well. It is a journey of self-discovery and self-improvement. Regularly engaging in self-reflection helps us maintain a healthy relationship with ourselves, navigate life's challenges with greater clarity and purpose, and cultivate a fulfilling and meaningful existence.

In conclusion, the art of self-reflection is a transformative practice that enhances personal growth, self-awareness, and well-being. By dedicating time to introspection, we gain valuable insights, understand ourselves better, and make conscious choices that align with our values and aspirations. Self-reflection is an ongoing journey of self-discovery and learning, empowering us to lead more purposeful and fulfilling lives.

Chapter 9: The power of visualization.

———

I n this chapter, we delve into the remarkable power of visualization and its impact on our lives. Visualization is the practice of creating vivid mental images or scenarios of desired outcomes, experiences, or goals. It is a powerful tool that harnesses the connection between our thoughts, emotions, and actions, allowing us to manifest our aspirations and shape our reality.

The human mind is a remarkable instrument that has the ability to imagine and create. Visualization taps into this innate capacity, leveraging the power of our imagination to influence our beliefs, attitudes, and behaviors. When we visualize our goals, dreams, or desired outcomes, we activate our subconscious mind and align our thoughts and emotions with the vision we hold.

One of the primary benefits of visualization is that it enhances focus and clarity. When we create mental images of what we want to achieve, we bring our goals and desires into sharp focus. This heightened focus directs our attention and energy towards the actions and opportunities that can propel us closer to our desired outcomes. Visualization acts as a guiding beacon, helping us stay on track and make decisions that align with our vision.

Visualization also plays a pivotal role in building confidence and belief in ourselves. By repeatedly visualizing ourselves successfully achieving our goals, we strengthen our self-belief and develop a positive mindset. When we vividly imagine ourselves overcoming obstacles and attaining our desired outcomes, we build resilience, determination, and a sense of self-efficacy. This increased confidence and belief in ourselves provide the motivation and drive to take consistent action towards our goals.

Furthermore, visualization taps into the power of the subconscious mind. Our subconscious mind is highly receptive to images and symbols. When we consistently visualize our desired outcomes, we send powerful messages to our subconscious, which then works in alignment with our conscious efforts to make our visions a reality. The subconscious mind acts as a powerful force that attracts opportunities, resources, and people who can support us in our journey.

Practicing visualization involves creating a clear mental image of our desired outcomes and engaging all our senses in the process. We can visualize the sights, sounds, smells, tastes, and even the emotions associated with our goals. The more detailed and vivid our visualizations, the more potent their impact. Regular practice strengthens the neural pathways associated with our visions, making them more ingrained in our subconscious and influencing our beliefs and behaviors.

In addition to visualizing the end result, it is beneficial to visualize the steps and actions required to achieve our goals. By visualizing ourselves taking focused and purposeful actions, we enhance our motivation and develop a sense of direction. This form of visualization helps us break down our goals into manageable tasks and provides a roadmap for success.

Visualization techniques can be combined with other practices to amplify their effectiveness. Affirmations, positive self-talk, and gratitude can complement visualization by reinforcing positive beliefs and emotions. Regularly affirming our capabilities and expressing gratitude for the progress we have made strengthens our visualization practice and cultivates a positive mindset.

It is important to note that visualization alone is not a substitute for action. While visualization sets the stage for success, it must be accompanied by consistent effort, dedication, and a willingness to adapt. Visualization serves as a powerful motivational tool that enhances our focus and belief, but ultimately, it is our actions that bring our visions to life.

In conclusion, the power of visualization is a transformative tool that can shape our beliefs, attitudes, and actions. By creating clear mental images of our goals and desired outcomes, we enhance our focus, belief, and motivation. Visualization aligns our conscious and subconscious mind, attracting opportunities and resources that support our journey. Combined with consistent action and a positive mindset, visualization empowers us to turn our dreams into reality and create the life we envision.

Chapter 10: Overcoming self-doubt.

———

In this chapter, we explore the pervasive issue of self-doubt and delve into strategies for overcoming it. Self-doubt is a common experience that can hinder our personal growth, limit our potential, and prevent us from pursuing our dreams and goals. By understanding the nature of self-doubt and implementing effective techniques, we can regain confidence, embrace our capabilities, and move forward with courage and resilience.

Self-doubt often stems from negative self-perception and fear of failure. It manifests as a voice of uncertainty and skepticism, questioning our abilities and worthiness. It can be triggered by past failures, comparison with others, or external criticism. However, self-doubt is not a reflection of our true capabilities, but rather a product of our thoughts and beliefs.

The first step in overcoming self-doubt is to develop self-awareness and recognize when self-doubt arises. Pay attention to the thoughts and emotions that accompany moments of self-doubt. By identifying these patterns, we can begin to challenge them and break free from their grip. It is crucial to remember that self-doubt is not an accurate reflection of our abilities, but rather a conditioned response that can be altered.

One powerful technique for overcoming self-doubt is reframing our thoughts. Instead of succumbing to negative self-talk, we can consciously choose to reframe our thoughts in a more positive and empowering manner. For example, when self-doubt creeps in and tells us, "I can't do this," we can counteract it with a positive affirmation such as, "I am capable and resourceful. I can handle any challenge that comes my way." By consistently reframing our thoughts, we create a new narrative that reinforces our confidence and self-belief.

Another effective strategy is to gather evidence of our past successes and accomplishments. Reflect on previous achievements and remind yourself of the challenges you have overcome. Keep a record of positive feedback, compliments, and testimonials from others. This collection of evidence serves as a reminder of your abilities and helps counteract the self-doubt that may arise.

Surrounding ourselves with a supportive network is crucial in overcoming self-doubt. Seek out mentors, friends, or family members who believe in you and can provide encouragement and guidance. Share your aspirations and fears with them, and allow their support to bolster your confidence. Their belief in you can serve as a powerful antidote to self-doubt and help you see your potential more clearly.

Taking action is another effective way to combat self-doubt. Often, self-doubt paralyzes us and prevents us from moving forward. However, by taking small, manageable steps towards our goals, we build momentum and prove to ourselves that we are capable of progress. Each small success serves as evidence of our abilities, eroding the self-doubt that may linger.

Cultivating self-compassion is essential in overcoming self-doubt. Treat yourself with kindness and understanding, especially when facing setbacks or challenges. Acknowledge that self-doubt is a natural part of the human experience and that everyone encounters it at some point. Be gentle with yourself and practice self-care, nurturing your well-being and resilience.

Developing a growth mindset is an effective long-term strategy for overcoming self-doubt. Embrace the belief that your abilities and intelligence can be developed through dedication and effort.

Emphasize the importance of learning and growth rather than focusing solely on outcomes. By adopting a growth mindset, you open yourself up to new possibilities and see challenges as opportunities for growth, rather than reasons for self-doubt.

Visualization can also be a powerful tool in overcoming self-doubt. Create mental images of yourself succeeding, confidently tackling challenges, and achieving your goals. Visualize the feeling of confidence and self-assurance that accompanies these successes. By regularly visualizing positive outcomes and reaffirming your belief in yourself, you can gradually diminish self-doubt and replace it with a sense of empowerment.

It is important to remember that overcoming self-doubt is not a linear process. There may be moments when self-doubt resurfaces, especially during times of uncertainty or when facing new challenges. During such times, it is crucial to practice self-compassion and remind yourself of the progress you have made.

Seeking professional help, such as working with a therapist or coach, can also be beneficial in overcoming self-doubt. They can provide guidance, support, and techniques tailored to your specific needs. A professional can help you identify underlying causes of self-doubt and provide strategies to overcome it effectively.

In conclusion, self-doubt is a common obstacle that can hinder personal growth and prevent us from reaching our full potential. By developing self-awareness, reframing our thoughts, gathering evidence of past successes, seeking support from others, taking action, cultivating self-compassion, adopting a growth mindset, and using visualization techniques, we can overcome self-doubt and embrace our true capabilities. Remember that self-doubt is not a reflection of your worth or abilities but merely a conditioned response that can be changed.

With persistence and the right strategies, you can break free from self-doubt and confidently pursue your goals and dreams.

Chapter 11: The art of listening and communication.

———

E ffective communication is a fundamental aspect of our personal and professional lives. In this chapter, we explore the art of listening and communication, and how developing these skills can enhance our relationships, improve understanding, and foster deeper connections with others.

Communication is a two-way process that involves both speaking and listening. While speaking allows us to express our thoughts and ideas, listening is equally important, as it enables us to understand others, validate their experiences, and build empathy. However, in our fast-paced world filled with distractions, true listening has become a rare and valuable skill.

Listening is more than just hearing words. It involves actively engaging with the speaker, paying attention to their verbal and non-verbal cues, and creating a safe and supportive space for them to express themselves. When we truly listen, we suspend judgment, set aside our own agenda, and give our undivided attention to the speaker.

One key aspect of effective listening is empathy. Empathy is the ability to understand and share the feelings of another person. By practicing empathy, we can connect with others on a deeper level and foster trust and understanding. This requires us to put ourselves in the speaker's shoes, validate their emotions, and respond with compassion and understanding.

Another important component of effective communication is non-verbal cues. Non-verbal communication includes facial expressions, body language, tone of voice, and gestures. Paying attention to these cues can provide valuable insights into the speaker's emotions and intentions. Additionally, our own non-verbal cues can greatly impact how our message is received. By maintaining eye contact, using open body language, and being mindful of our tone, we can convey respect, openness, and receptiveness.

Active listening involves utilizing specific techniques to demonstrate our engagement and understanding. Reflective listening, for example, involves paraphrasing and summarizing the speaker's message to ensure that we have correctly understood their perspective. This not only shows that we are actively listening but also allows the speaker to clarify any misconceptions.

Another technique is asking open-ended questions to encourage the speaker to elaborate and delve deeper into their thoughts and feelings. This promotes a more meaningful and authentic conversation. Additionally, practicing patience and allowing for pauses and silences can create a comfortable space for the speaker to gather their thoughts and express themselves fully.

Effective communication also involves being aware of our own communication style and adapting it to different situations and individuals. Some individuals may respond better to direct and assertive communication, while others may prefer a more gentle and supportive approach. Being adaptable and flexible in our communication allows us to connect with others more effectively and create a harmonious and collaborative environment.

Furthermore, communication is not only about expressing our own thoughts and feelings but also actively seeking to understand others. This requires genuine curiosity and a willingness to explore different perspectives. By fostering an inclusive and open-minded approach to communication, we can bridge gaps, resolve conflicts, and cultivate a sense of unity and understanding.

In our increasingly digital world, it is important to recognize the impact of technology on communication. While technology has made communication more accessible, it can also hinder meaningful connections. It is essential to strike a balance between online and offline communication, ensuring that we prioritize face-to-face interactions and actively listen to those around us.

In conclusion, the art of listening and communication is a vital skill set that enhances our relationships, deepens understanding, and cultivates empathy. By practicing active listening, utilizing non-verbal cues, demonstrating empathy, employing reflective listening techniques, adapting our communication style, seeking to understand others, and maintaining a balance between online and offline communication, we can become effective communicators and create meaningful connections with others. Remember, effective communication starts with listening, and by truly listening, we can foster understanding, empathy, and harmony in our interactions.

Chapter 12: Constructive conflict resolution.

─────

Conflict is a natural part of human interactions, and learning how to navigate and resolve conflicts in a constructive manner is essential for personal growth and maintaining healthy relationships. In this chapter, we explore the art of constructive conflict resolution and the strategies that can help us resolve conflicts effectively while fostering understanding, empathy, and collaboration.

Conflict arises when individuals have differing opinions, needs, or expectations. It can occur in various settings, including personal relationships, workplaces, and social environments. While conflicts can be challenging and uncomfortable, they also present an opportunity for growth, learning, and strengthening relationships if approached with the right mindset and strategies.

The first step in constructive conflict resolution is to develop self-awareness and emotional intelligence. Understanding our own emotions, triggers, and biases allows us to approach conflicts with a calm and rational mindset. It is important to acknowledge and manage our emotions effectively, as they can influence our communication and decision-making during conflict situations.

Active listening is a critical component of resolving conflicts constructively. It involves giving our full attention to the other person, suspending judgment, and seeking to understand their perspective. By listening empathetically and without interruption, we create a safe space for the other person to express their thoughts and feelings. This fosters mutual respect and lays the foundation for effective communication and problem-solving.

Expressing ourselves assertively is another key aspect of constructive conflict resolution. Assertiveness involves clearly and respectfully communicating our needs, concerns, and boundaries. It is important to use "I" statements to express our feelings and avoid blaming or accusing the other person. By expressing ourselves assertively, we promote open and honest communication, creating an environment where conflicts can be addressed constructively.

Finding common ground and areas of agreement is crucial in resolving conflicts. It is helpful to focus on shared interests and goals, rather than getting stuck on differences. By identifying common objectives, we can work collaboratively towards finding mutually beneficial solutions. This requires a willingness to compromise and seek win-win outcomes, where both parties' needs are met to some extent.

Effective problem-solving techniques, such as brainstorming and considering multiple perspectives, can facilitate constructive conflict resolution. Brainstorming allows for the generation of creative solutions and encourages collaboration. It is important to separate the problem from the person and approach the situation with a solution-oriented mindset. By exploring different options and perspectives, we can find innovative solutions that address the underlying issues causing the conflict.

Maintaining respect and empathy throughout the conflict resolution process is essential. It is important to treat the other person with dignity, even when disagreements are heated. Avoid personal attacks and focus on the issue at hand. By demonstrating empathy and understanding, we create an environment where both parties feel heard and valued, increasing the chances of finding a resolution that satisfies everyone involved.

In some cases, seeking the assistance of a neutral third party can be beneficial in resolving conflicts. Mediation or facilitation can provide an unbiased perspective and help guide the process towards a mutually agreeable resolution. A mediator can help create a safe and structured environment for open communication, ensuring that both parties have an equal opportunity to express their concerns and work towards a resolution.

Lastly, it is important to reflect on conflicts as learning opportunities. Each conflict presents a chance to understand ourselves and others better, develop stronger communication skills, and improve our relationships. By approaching conflicts with a growth mindset, we can extract valuable lessons and use them to navigate future conflicts more effectively.

In conclusion, constructive conflict resolution is an essential skill for personal and interpersonal growth. By developing self-awareness, practicing active listening, expressing ourselves assertively, finding common ground, employing effective problem-solving techniques, maintaining respect and empathy, seeking assistance when needed, and viewing conflicts as learning opportunities, we can resolve conflicts in a constructive manner. Constructive conflict resolution promotes understanding, strengthens relationships, and fosters a collaborative and harmonious environment. It requires patience, open-mindedness, and a willingness to engage in honest and respectful dialogue.

It is important to remember that conflicts are not inherently negative or destructive. They can provide an opportunity for individuals to express their needs and perspectives, leading to greater understanding and growth. By approaching conflicts with a mindset focused on resolution rather than winning or proving oneself right, we can create an atmosphere conducive to finding mutually beneficial solutions.

During the conflict resolution process, it is essential to manage emotions effectively. Emotions can run high during conflicts, and if left unchecked, they can hinder productive communication and problem-solving. Taking breaks when needed, practicing self-care, and using calming techniques such as deep breathing or mindfulness can help maintain emotional balance and clarity.

Resolving conflicts constructively also requires a commitment to active problem-solving. This involves identifying the root causes of the conflict and exploring potential solutions that address those underlying issues. Brainstorming, considering alternative perspectives, and engaging in open and honest dialogue can lead to creative and mutually satisfying resolutions.

Conflict resolution often involves compromise and finding middle ground. It is important to understand that compromising does not mean sacrificing one's values or needs entirely. Rather, it involves finding a balance that respects the interests and concerns of all parties involved. By seeking win-win outcomes, conflicts can be resolved in a manner that preserves relationships and fosters cooperation.

Additionally, effective communication skills play a vital role in constructive conflict resolution. Clear and respectful communication helps to avoid misunderstandings and ensures that all parties are on the same page. It is important to use "I" statements to express feelings and needs without blaming or attacking others. Active listening, paraphrasing, and seeking clarification are also crucial in promoting understanding and preventing miscommunication.

Lastly, it is essential to review and evaluate the resolution process after conflicts have been resolved. Reflecting on the outcomes, identifying lessons learned, and implementing any necessary changes can help prevent future conflicts and promote continuous personal and interpersonal growth.

In conclusion, constructive conflict resolution is a valuable skill that empowers individuals to navigate conflicts in a way that promotes understanding, collaboration, and growth. By developing self-awareness, practicing active listening, expressing oneself assertively, seeking common ground, employing effective problem-solving techniques, managing emotions, maintaining respectful communication, and reflecting on the resolution process, conflicts can be transformed into opportunities for positive change. With dedication and a commitment to constructive resolution, individuals can cultivate healthier relationships and contribute to a more harmonious and productive environment.

Chapter 13: Cultivating empathy and compassion.

———

E mpathy and compassion are powerful qualities that have the ability to transform our relationships, enhance our understanding of others, and foster a more compassionate and inclusive society. In this chapter, we explore the importance of cultivating empathy and compassion and provide practical strategies to develop these qualities in our everyday lives.

Empathy is the ability to understand and share the feelings of another person. It goes beyond sympathy, which involves feeling sorry for someone's situation, and instead, allows us to step into their shoes and truly connect with their experiences. Empathy involves active listening, observing non-verbal cues, and validating the emotions of others. By practicing empathy, we can build deeper connections, strengthen relationships, and create a supportive and compassionate environment.

To cultivate empathy, it is essential to develop self-awareness. Understanding our own emotions, biases, and judgments allows us to approach others with an open mind and genuine curiosity. It is important to recognize and challenge any preconceived notions or stereotypes that may hinder our ability to empathize with others. By embracing diversity and actively seeking to understand different perspectives, we can broaden our empathetic capacity.

Active listening is a fundamental skill in cultivating empathy. By giving our full attention to others, suspending judgment, and truly listening to their words and emotions, we create a safe space for them to express themselves. It is important to focus on the speaker's perspective, ask open-ended questions to encourage deeper sharing, and reflect back their thoughts and feelings to show understanding and empathy.

Another key aspect of cultivating empathy is developing emotional intelligence. Emotional intelligence involves recognizing and managing our own emotions, as well as understanding the emotions of others. By being attuned to the emotional states of those around us, we can respond with empathy and compassion. This includes being aware of both verbal and non-verbal cues, such as facial expressions, body language, and tone of voice.

Compassion is closely linked to empathy and involves a genuine concern for the well-being of others. It is the willingness to extend kindness, understanding, and support to those who may be suffering or in need. Cultivating compassion involves practicing acts of kindness and empathy on a daily basis. This can be as simple as offering a listening ear, providing a helping hand, or showing genuine care and concern for others.

One effective strategy for cultivating empathy and compassion is to engage in perspective-taking exercises. This involves imagining oneself in another person's situation and considering their thoughts, feelings, and experiences. This exercise helps to broaden our understanding and deepen our empathy. Reading books, watching movies or documentaries, or engaging in diverse conversations can also expose us to different perspectives and enhance our empathetic capacity.

Practicing self-compassion is equally important in cultivating empathy and compassion. It involves extending the same kindness and understanding to ourselves that we offer to others. By nurturing a positive and compassionate relationship with ourselves, we are better able to empathize with the struggles and challenges faced by others. Self-compassion involves acknowledging our own limitations, being forgiving of our mistakes, and practicing self-care.

Engaging in acts of service and volunteering is another powerful way to cultivate empathy and compassion. By actively helping others, we develop a deeper understanding of their needs and challenges. Volunteering allows us to contribute to the well-being of others while fostering a sense of connection and gratitude.

In conclusion, cultivating empathy and compassion is essential for building meaningful relationships, promoting understanding, and creating a compassionate society. By developing self-awareness, practicing active listening, engaging in perspective-taking exercises, nurturing self-compassion, and engaging in acts of service, we can strengthen our empathetic capacity and make a positive impact in the lives of others. Cultivating empathy and compassion is a lifelong journey that requires practice, but the rewards are immeasurable

Chapter 14: Building healthy relationships.

———

B uilding and maintaining healthy relationships is a fundamental aspect of personal growth and well-being. In this chapter, we explore the key elements of fostering healthy relationships and provide practical strategies to cultivate meaningful connections with others.

Healthy relationships are built on a foundation of mutual respect, trust, and effective communication. They involve a balance of give-and-take, support, and understanding. Whether it is a romantic partnership, friendship, or professional relationship, the principles of building healthy relationships remain consistent.

One essential element of healthy relationships is effective communication. Clear and open communication allows for the expression of thoughts, feelings, and needs, while also promoting understanding and resolving conflicts. It is important to actively listen to others, validate their perspectives, and express oneself honestly and assertively. By practicing active communication, misunderstandings can be minimized, and connections can be deepened.

Trust is another crucial component of healthy relationships. Trust is built over time through consistent and reliable actions. It involves being honest, keeping commitments, and respecting boundaries. Trust allows individuals to feel secure and safe within the relationship, fostering a sense of intimacy and connection. Building trust requires vulnerability and a willingness to be open and transparent with one another.

Respect is the foundation of any healthy relationship. It involves valuing each other's opinions, boundaries, and autonomy. Respecting differences and embracing diversity is also essential in cultivating a harmonious and inclusive relationship. Treating each other with kindness, empathy, and consideration creates an environment where both parties feel valued and appreciated.

Boundaries play a vital role in maintaining healthy relationships. Setting and respecting personal boundaries ensures that each individual's needs and limits are honored. Boundaries help establish a sense of self-identity and protect against feelings of being overwhelmed or taken advantage of. Clear communication and mutual respect are crucial when discussing and maintaining boundaries within a relationship.

In addition to effective communication and trust, healthy relationships thrive on emotional support. Being there for one another during both the joys and challenges of life creates a sense of closeness and solidarity. Offering empathy, validation, and encouragement strengthens the bond between individuals. Active listening and expressing empathy allows for a deeper understanding of each other's emotions and experiences.

Conflict resolution is an inevitable part of any relationship, and handling conflicts in a healthy and constructive manner is vital. It involves listening to each other's perspectives, finding common ground, and seeking win-win solutions. Resolving conflicts with respect, empathy, and open-mindedness strengthens the relationship and fosters growth and understanding.

Nurturing healthy relationships also requires investing time and effort. Spending quality time together, engaging in shared activities, and creating meaningful memories help to build a strong foundation. It is important to prioritize the relationship and demonstrate commitment through consistent actions and gestures of love and appreciation.

Self-reflection is a valuable practice when building healthy relationships. Taking the time to examine one's own beliefs, values, and communication patterns allows for personal growth and self-improvement. Recognizing and addressing any unhealthy patterns or unresolved issues from the past contributes to building healthier and more fulfilling relationships in the present.

Lastly, it is important to remember that healthy relationships require ongoing maintenance and effort. Regular check-ins, honest conversations, and a willingness to adapt and grow together contribute to the longevity and strength of the relationship. Celebrating successes, supporting each other's goals, and demonstrating gratitude further nurture the connection.

In conclusion, building and maintaining healthy relationships is a lifelong endeavor that requires commitment, effective communication, trust, respect, and empathy. By investing in open and honest communication, fostering trust, respecting boundaries, providing emotional support, resolving conflicts constructively, spending quality time together, engaging in self-reflection, and demonstrating commitment, individuals can cultivate meaningful and fulfilling connections with others. Healthy relationships contribute to personal happiness, growth, and overall well-being.

Chapter 15: Networking for personal and professional growth.

———

Networking is a powerful tool for personal and professional growth, opening doors to new opportunities, connections, and knowledge. In this chapter, we explore the importance of networking and provide practical strategies to build and leverage networks for personal and professional advancement.

Networking involves establishing and nurturing relationships with individuals who share similar interests, goals, or professional fields. It is a proactive approach to connecting with others, fostering mutually beneficial relationships, and expanding one's circle of influence. Whether you are seeking career opportunities, professional advice, or personal development, networking can be a valuable asset.

One of the key benefits of networking is access to a broader pool of knowledge and expertise. By connecting with individuals from different backgrounds and industries, you gain exposure to diverse perspectives, insights, and ideas. Engaging in conversations, attending events, and participating in online communities enable you to tap into the collective wisdom and experiences of others.

Networking also provides opportunities for collaboration and partnerships. By building relationships with like-minded individuals, you can identify potential collaborators, mentors, or co-founders for projects or business ventures. Collaborative efforts not only enhance creativity and innovation but also allow for the sharing of resources and skills, leading to mutual growth and success.

A strong network can also serve as a support system. During challenging times or career transitions, having a network of trusted individuals can provide guidance, advice, and emotional support. Networking allows you to surround yourself with individuals who understand your journey, share similar aspirations, and can offer encouragement and assistance when needed.

When it comes to professional growth, networking plays a crucial role in career advancement. Many job opportunities arise through personal connections and referrals rather than traditional job postings. By actively networking within your industry or desired field, you increase your visibility and access to hidden job markets. Building relationships with professionals in positions of influence can also lead to mentorship or sponsorship opportunities, opening doors to career progression.

Effective networking involves both online and offline efforts. Online platforms such as LinkedIn, professional forums, and social media groups provide opportunities to connect with professionals worldwide. Actively engaging in online discussions, sharing valuable content, and reaching out to individuals of interest can help establish meaningful connections. However, it is important to also prioritize face-to-face interactions by attending industry conferences, networking events, and local meetups. Building authentic connections in person allows for deeper relationships and a stronger sense of trust.

To make the most out of networking opportunities, it is crucial to approach networking with a genuine and giving mindset. Focus on building relationships rather than solely seeking personal gain. Actively listen to others, show interest in their work or goals, and offer support or assistance when possible. Networking is a two-way street, and by providing value to others, you enhance your own reputation and create a positive impression.

Building a strong network requires consistent effort and nurturing. Regularly follow up with contacts, maintain open lines of communication, and seek opportunities to connect and collaborate. Remember to express gratitude and appreciation for the support and guidance received from your network. Building strong relationships takes time and effort, but the benefits are immeasurable.

Lastly, it is important to embrace diversity and inclusivity in your network. Connect with individuals from different backgrounds, cultures, and perspectives. By diversifying your network, you expand your horizons, challenge your own assumptions, and gain a more comprehensive understanding of the world. Embracing diversity fosters creativity, innovation, and cultural intelligence, which are highly valued in today's interconnected world.

In conclusion, networking is a powerful tool for personal and professional growth. By actively engaging in networking activities, you can expand your knowledge, form collaborations, gain support, and access new opportunities. Approach networking with a genuine and giving mindset, both online and offline. Cultivate relationships, nurture connections, and embrace diversity within your network.

Chapter 16: Embracing a healthy lifestyle.

———

A healthy lifestyle is the foundation for overall well-being and personal growth. It encompasses various aspects of our lives, including physical health, mental well-being, nutrition, and self-care. In this chapter, we explore the importance of embracing a healthy lifestyle and provide practical strategies to incorporate healthy habits into our daily lives.

Physical health is a fundamental pillar of a healthy lifestyle. Regular exercise and physical activity not only improve our physical fitness but also boost our mood, enhance cognitive function, and reduce the risk of chronic diseases. Finding an exercise routine that suits your preferences and interests is key to maintaining consistency. Whether it's going for a jog, practicing yoga, or engaging in team sports, find activities that bring you joy and make them a regular part of your routine.

In addition to exercise, prioritizing proper nutrition is vital for overall health. Consuming a balanced diet that includes a variety of fruits, vegetables, whole grains, lean proteins, and healthy fats provides the necessary nutrients for our bodies to function optimally. Avoiding excessive sugar, processed foods, and unhealthy fats can help reduce the risk of obesity, heart disease, and other health conditions. It's important to listen to your body's hunger and fullness cues, practice mindful eating, and make informed choices about the food you consume.

Mental well-being is equally important in maintaining a healthy lifestyle. Stress management techniques such as meditation, deep breathing exercises, and mindfulness practices can help reduce anxiety and promote emotional balance. Engaging in activities that bring you joy and relaxation, such as hobbies, creative outlets, or spending time in nature, can also contribute to mental well-being. Prioritizing sleep is crucial as well, as it allows our bodies and minds to rest and recharge, promoting optimal cognitive function and emotional stability.

Self-care is a fundamental component of a healthy lifestyle. Taking time for oneself, engaging in activities that promote relaxation and self-reflection, and setting boundaries to protect personal well-being are essential. Self-care practices can include anything from taking a bubble bath, reading a book, practicing gratitude, or engaging in self-reflection exercises. It is important to tune in to your own needs and prioritize self-care activities that replenish your energy and nurture your soul.

Building and maintaining strong social connections is another aspect of a healthy lifestyle. Surrounding yourself with a supportive network of friends and loved ones provides emotional support, a sense of belonging, and contributes to overall happiness and well-being. Engaging in meaningful conversations, spending quality time together, and nurturing relationships are essential for personal growth and a fulfilling life.

Embracing a healthy lifestyle also includes taking care of our environment. Being mindful of our ecological footprint, practicing sustainable habits, and contributing to a clean and healthy environment benefits not only ourselves but also future generations. This can involve recycling, conserving energy and water, reducing waste, and making environmentally conscious choices in our daily lives.

Maintaining a healthy lifestyle requires commitment, consistency, and a positive mindset. It's important to set realistic goals, make gradual changes, and celebrate small victories along the way. Remember that a healthy lifestyle is not about perfection but about making conscious choices that support your overall well-being.

Seeking professional guidance, such as consulting with a healthcare provider, nutritionist, or mental health professional, can provide additional support and guidance on your journey towards a healthy lifestyle. These experts can offer personalized advice and help tailor a plan that suits your individual needs and goals.

In conclusion, embracing a healthy lifestyle is a holistic approach to personal growth and well-being. By prioritizing physical health, mental well-being, nutrition, self-care, social connections, and environmental consciousness, we can create a foundation for a vibrant and fulfilling life. Incorporating healthy habits into our daily routines, seeking support when needed, and maintaining

Chapter 17: The importance of exercise and fitness.

———

E xercise and fitness play a crucial role in our overall well-being and personal growth. In this chapter, we explore the significance of exercise and fitness, highlighting the physical, mental, and emotional benefits they provide. We also provide practical strategies to incorporate exercise into our daily lives and develop a sustainable fitness routine.

Physical health is one of the primary reasons why exercise and fitness are essential. Regular physical activity helps maintain a healthy weight, improves cardiovascular health, strengthens muscles and bones, and enhances overall physical fitness. Engaging in exercises that target different muscle groups, such as strength training, cardiovascular activities, and flexibility exercises, helps promote a balanced and well-rounded fitness level. Additionally, regular exercise can boost our immune system, reduce the risk of chronic diseases such as heart disease and diabetes, and improve longevity.

Exercise also has significant mental and emotional benefits. When we engage in physical activity, our bodies release endorphins, which are natural chemicals that promote feelings of happiness and reduce stress and anxiety. Regular exercise has been linked to improved mood, reduced symptoms of depression, and enhanced cognitive function. It can help increase focus, concentration, and memory, contributing to better overall mental well-being. Exercise also provides a healthy outlet for managing stress and can serve as a form of self-care, allowing us to take a break from our daily routines and rejuvenate both physically and mentally.

Furthermore, exercise and fitness play a vital role in personal growth and self-confidence. As we challenge ourselves physically and achieve fitness goals, we develop a sense of accomplishment and self-efficacy. Regular exercise helps improve body image and self-esteem, promoting a positive self-image and increased self-confidence. Through physical activity, we also learn discipline, perseverance, and goal-setting, which can be applied to other areas of our lives, leading to personal growth and success.

Incorporating exercise into our daily lives requires commitment and planning. It is essential to find activities that we enjoy and that align with our preferences and goals. Whether it's participating in team sports, going for a jog, cycling, swimming, or practicing yoga, finding activities that resonate with us increases the likelihood of sticking to a regular exercise routine. It's also important to mix up our workouts to avoid boredom and keep ourselves motivated. Trying new activities or varying the intensity and duration of our workouts can help keep things exciting and challenging.

Making exercise a priority in our daily schedules is crucial for maintaining consistency. Setting specific goals, such as exercising a certain number of days per week or achieving specific fitness milestones, provides direction and motivation. Scheduling exercise sessions in advance, treating them as non-negotiable appointments, and finding an exercise buddy or joining a fitness community can help hold us accountable and provide additional support and motivation.

It's important to listen to our bodies and exercise in a safe and responsible manner. Starting slowly and gradually increasing the intensity and duration of our workouts can help prevent injuries and avoid burnout. Proper warm-up and cool-down routines, along with stretching exercises, can improve flexibility and reduce the risk of muscle strain. If necessary, consulting with a healthcare professional or working with a qualified fitness trainer can provide guidance on proper form, technique, and individualized exercise programs.

Incorporating exercise into our daily routines can be done in various ways. Taking the stairs instead of the elevator, walking or biking to work, incorporating physical activity breaks during sedentary periods, and using fitness apps or wearable devices to track our progress can all contribute to a more active lifestyle. The key is to find opportunities to move and be physically active throughout the day, even if it's in small increments.

In conclusion, exercise and fitness are essential components of a healthy and fulfilling life. Engaging in regular physical activity not only improves our physical health but also enhances mental well-being.

Chapter 18: Nutrition and energy levels.

———

Nutrition plays a fundamental role in our overall well-being and energy levels. In this chapter, we explore the importance of nutrition in sustaining high energy levels and promoting optimal physical and mental performance. We also provide practical strategies for incorporating a balanced and nutritious diet into our daily lives.

The food we consume serves as fuel for our bodies, providing the energy necessary for daily activities, mental focus, and physical performance. Optimal nutrition ensures that our bodies receive the essential nutrients, vitamins, and minerals required for proper functioning. A well-balanced diet provides a steady supply of energy throughout the day, preventing energy crashes and promoting sustained productivity.

Carbohydrates, proteins, and fats are the macronutrients that supply the majority of our energy. Carbohydrates are the body's preferred source of fuel, supplying glucose that is converted into energy. Complex carbohydrates, found in whole grains, fruits, and vegetables, provide a slow and steady release of energy, while simple carbohydrates, found in sugary foods and beverages, offer a quick but short-lived burst of energy. Including a mix of complex carbohydrates in our diet helps maintain stable energy levels throughout the day.

Proteins play a vital role in repairing and building tissues, including muscles, and are essential for maintaining proper immune function. Incorporating lean sources of protein, such as poultry, fish, beans, and tofu, into our meals helps provide a sustained release of energy and promotes satiety. Including a variety of protein sources in our diet ensures that we receive all essential amino acids necessary for optimal health.

Fats are another important energy source and are involved in various bodily functions. Healthy fats, such as those found in avocados, nuts, seeds, and olive oil, provide sustained energy and help support brain function. It's important to choose healthy fats over saturated and trans fats, which can increase the risk of cardiovascular diseases and lead to low energy levels.

In addition to macronutrients, consuming a wide range of micronutrients is essential for maintaining energy levels. Vitamins and minerals, such as iron, B vitamins, magnesium, and vitamin C, play key roles in energy metabolism and the production of energy molecules in our cells. Including a variety of fruits, vegetables, whole grains, and lean proteins in our diet ensures that we receive an adequate supply of these essential nutrients.

Hydration is also crucial for maintaining energy levels. Dehydration can lead to fatigue and decreased cognitive function. It's important to drink plenty of water throughout the day and stay hydrated, especially during physical activity or in hot weather.

To incorporate a balanced and nutritious diet into our daily lives, it's helpful to plan our meals and snacks in advance. Having a well-stocked pantry with wholesome foods allows for easy access to nutritious options. Prioritizing whole, unprocessed foods and minimizing the consumption of processed and sugary foods helps ensure that we receive the necessary nutrients without unnecessary additives or empty calories.

Eating regular meals and snacks throughout the day helps maintain stable blood sugar levels and prevents energy crashes. Including a mix of complex carbohydrates, proteins, and healthy fats in each meal promotes balanced energy release and keeps us feeling satisfied. It's also important to listen to our bodies' hunger and fullness cues and eat mindfully, savoring each bite and being present during meal times.

Incorporating a variety of colorful fruits and vegetables into our meals ensures a wide range of vitamins, minerals, and antioxidants. These powerful plant compounds support our overall health, enhance our immune system, and provide the necessary nutrients for sustained energy.

Lastly, it's important to approach nutrition with a balanced and flexible mindset. Allowing for occasional indulgences and enjoying our favorite foods in moderation promotes a healthy relationship with food. Avoiding strict diets or restrictive eating patterns helps.

Chapter 19: Stress management and relaxation techniques.

———

In today's fast-paced and demanding world, stress has become a common part of our lives. In this chapter, we explore the importance of stress management and relaxation techniques for our overall well-being. We provide practical strategies to help reduce stress levels and promote relaxation, leading to a more balanced and fulfilling life.

Stress can have detrimental effects on our physical, mental, and emotional health. It can lead to increased blood pressure, weakened immune system, disrupted sleep patterns, and feelings of anxiety and overwhelm. Therefore, it is crucial to develop effective stress management techniques to mitigate the negative impact of stress on our well-being.

One of the key strategies for managing stress is practicing relaxation techniques. These techniques help activate the body's relaxation response, counteracting the physiological changes associated with stress. Deep breathing exercises, such as diaphragmatic breathing or box breathing, help calm the nervous system and induce a state of relaxation. By focusing on our breath and consciously slowing down our breathing, we can reduce stress and promote a sense of calm.

Meditation and mindfulness practices are also effective tools for stress management. Taking a few minutes each day to sit in silence, observe our thoughts without judgment, and cultivate a sense of present-moment awareness can significantly reduce stress levels. Mindfulness can be incorporated into various activities, such as mindful eating, walking, or even engaging in daily chores. By bringing our full attention to the present moment, we can let go of worries and anxieties, leading to a greater sense of peace and well-being.

Physical activity and exercise are not only beneficial for our physical health but also play a crucial role in stress management. Engaging in regular physical activity helps release endorphins, the body's natural feel-good hormones, and reduces stress hormones such as cortisol. Whether it's going for a walk, practicing yoga, or engaging in a high-intensity workout, finding an exercise routine that suits our preferences and schedule can significantly reduce stress levels and promote relaxation.

Engaging in hobbies and activities that bring joy and relaxation can also help manage stress. Whether it's reading, listening to music, painting, gardening, or playing an instrument, dedicating time to activities we enjoy allows us to disconnect from stressors and recharge mentally and emotionally. It's important to prioritize these activities and make them a regular part of our routine to ensure consistent stress relief.

Social support is another crucial aspect of stress management. Talking to trusted friends, family members, or a therapist can provide an outlet for expressing our feelings and concerns. Sharing our experiences and receiving support from others can help alleviate stress and provide a fresh perspective on challenging situations. Building and nurturing positive relationships and connections with others is essential for our overall well-being and stress management.

Creating a balanced and supportive lifestyle is important in managing stress. Prioritizing self-care activities, such as getting enough sleep, eating a nutritious diet, and engaging in activities that promote relaxation, can help reduce stress levels and increase resilience. Setting realistic goals, managing time effectively, and practicing good time management skills can also help reduce stress associated with work or personal responsibilities.

It's important to be aware of our stress triggers and develop healthy coping mechanisms. Journaling, practicing gratitude, and engaging in positive self-talk are effective ways to manage stress and cultivate a positive mindset. Additionally, learning to say "no" when necessary, setting boundaries, and practicing self-compassion are essential in managing stress and preventing burnout.

In conclusion, stress management and relaxation techniques are vital for maintaining a healthy and balanced life. By incorporating relaxation techniques, engaging in regular physical activity, seeking social support, and creating a supportive lifestyle, we can effectively manage stress and promote overall well-being. Taking time to prioritize self-care and relaxation not only benefits ourselves but also allows us to show up as

Chapter 20: Sleep and its impact on performance.

―――――

Sleep is a fundamental aspect of our lives, playing a crucial role in our overall well-being and performance. In this chapter, we explore the importance of sleep and its impact on our physical, mental, and cognitive abilities. We also provide practical strategies to optimize sleep quality and quantity for enhanced performance.

Sleep is not merely a period of rest; it is a complex process that allows our bodies and minds to rejuvenate and restore. During sleep, the body undergoes important physiological processes, such as tissue repair, muscle growth, and the release of growth hormones. The brain also consolidates memories, processes information, and regulates mood during sleep. Thus, quality sleep is essential for maintaining optimal physical and mental health.

One of the primary ways sleep impacts performance is through its effect on cognitive abilities. Sufficient and restorative sleep is associated with improved attention, concentration, problem-solving skills, and creativity. It enhances our ability to learn and retain information, allowing for better academic or work performance. Lack of sleep, on the other hand, can impair cognitive function, leading to decreased productivity, difficulty concentrating, and reduced decision-making abilities.

Sleep also plays a critical role in physical performance and athletic abilities. During sleep, the body repairs and strengthens muscles, allowing for optimal physical recovery. It also regulates the release of hormones involved in muscle growth and repair. Athletes who prioritize sleep experience improved reaction time, increased speed, enhanced endurance, and reduced risk of injuries. Proper sleep hygiene is particularly crucial for athletes and individuals involved in physical training.

Furthermore, sleep has a profound impact on our mood, emotional well-being, and overall mental health. Adequate sleep helps regulate mood, reduces feelings of irritability and anxiety, and enhances emotional resilience. On the other hand, chronic sleep deprivation is associated with an increased risk of developing mental health conditions, such as depression and anxiety disorders.

To optimize sleep quality and quantity, it's important to practice good sleep hygiene. Establishing a consistent sleep schedule by going to bed and waking up at the same time each day helps regulate the body's internal clock and promotes a more restful sleep. Creating a conducive sleep environment, characterized by a cool, dark, and quiet room, can help minimize disruptions and enhance sleep quality.

Engaging in a relaxing bedtime routine can signal the body that it's time to wind down and prepare for sleep. Activities such as taking a warm bath, practicing relaxation techniques like deep breathing or meditation, and avoiding stimulating activities, such as using electronic devices or consuming caffeine, before bedtime can promote a more restful sleep.

Developing healthy sleep habits includes creating an optimal sleep environment and establishing a pre-sleep routine. It's also important to prioritize sleep and allocate sufficient time for rest. Most adults require between 7-9 hours of sleep per night, although individual sleep needs may vary. It's crucial to listen to our bodies and adjust our sleep duration accordingly.

In addition to good sleep hygiene practices, adopting a healthy lifestyle can contribute to better sleep. Regular physical activity during the day promotes better sleep quality at night. However, vigorous exercise close to bedtime may have a stimulating effect, so it's advisable to finish exercising a few hours before sleep.

Nutrition also plays a role in sleep quality. Consuming a balanced diet that includes foods rich in sleep-promoting nutrients, such as magnesium and tryptophan, can support a more restful sleep. Avoiding heavy meals, spicy or greasy foods, and excessive fluid intake before bedtime can prevent discomfort and interruptions during the night.

For individuals who struggle with persistent sleep difficulties, it may be beneficial to consult a healthcare professional or sleep specialist. They can help identify and address underlying sleep disorders or provide guidance on strategies such as cognitive-behavioral therapy for insomnia (CBT-I).

Chapter 21: Identifying strengths and talents.

———

U nderstanding our strengths and talents is essential for personal and professional growth. In this chapter, we explore the importance of identifying and leveraging our unique strengths and talents. We provide practical strategies to help uncover and develop these qualities, enabling us to maximize our potential and achieve success.

Our strengths and talents are the natural abilities, skills, and characteristics that come to us effortlessly and give us a sense of fulfillment and satisfaction. They are the areas where we excel and have the potential to make a significant impact. By recognizing and nurturing our strengths, we can enhance our self-confidence, boost our motivation, and improve our performance in various aspects of life.

Identifying our strengths begins with self-reflection and self-awareness. Taking the time to reflect on our past experiences and achievements can reveal patterns of success and activities that bring us joy and fulfillment. What tasks or projects have we excelled in? What activities do we find ourselves naturally drawn to? Exploring these questions can provide valuable insights into our inherent strengths and talents.

Feedback from others is another valuable resource for identifying our strengths. Seeking input from trusted friends, family members, mentors, or colleagues can provide an external perspective on our unique qualities and abilities. They may have observed specific talents or strengths in us that we may not have recognized ourselves. Their insights can help us gain a deeper understanding of our potential and areas where we can thrive.

Personality assessments and psychometric tests can also be useful tools for uncovering our strengths. These assessments provide structured evaluations of our personality traits, preferences, and aptitudes. They can highlight areas where we have a natural inclination or excel, giving us a clear picture of our unique strengths and talents.

Once we have identified our strengths, it's important to develop and nurture them. Building on our strengths allows us to leverage them to achieve personal and professional goals. Here are some strategies to develop and maximize our strengths:

1.Practice and refine: Just like any skill, our strengths can be further honed through practice and continuous learning. Engaging in activities that allow us to apply and develop our strengths helps us become even more proficient in those areas.

2.Seek opportunities: Actively seek out opportunities that align with our strengths. Whether it's choosing projects at work, joining organizations or communities that value and utilize your strengths, or pursuing hobbies that allow you to express your talents, actively seeking opportunities to apply your strengths will help you grow and excel.

3.Surround yourself with support: Surround yourself with people who appreciate and value your strengths. Collaborating with individuals who complement your strengths can create synergistic relationships and amplify your collective abilities. Seek mentors and coaches who can provide guidance and support in further developing your strengths.

4.Continuous learning: Keep abreast of developments and trends in areas related to your strengths. Stay curious and open to new ideas and approaches. By continuously learning and expanding your knowledge, you can stay at the forefront of your field and continue to enhance your strengths.

5.Embrace challenges: Don't shy away from challenges that allow you to stretch and apply your strengths in new and different ways. Embracing challenges helps you develop resilience, problem-solving skills, and a deeper understanding of your strengths.

It's important to note that identifying strengths doesn't mean ignoring weaknesses. While focusing on our strengths is crucial, it's also necessary to address areas where we may have limitations. Recognizing our weaknesses allows us to take steps to improve or find support in those areas, ensuring a well-rounded and balanced approach to personal and professional growth.

In conclusion, identifying and leveraging our strengths and talents is key to personal and professional success. By understanding our unique qualities, we can build on our strengths, seek opportunities that align with them, and continuously develop and refine our abilities. Embracing our strengths allows us to bring our best selves to various aspects of our lives, whether it's our career, relationships, or personal pursuits.

When we operate from a place of strength, we not only experience greater fulfillment and satisfaction but also make a more significant impact in the areas that matter to us. By recognizing and capitalizing on our strengths, we can contribute our unique talents and abilities to the world, creating positive change and achieving our goals.

Moreover, identifying our strengths can help us make informed decisions about our career path and professional development. When we align our work with our strengths, we are more likely to find enjoyment, meaning, and success in our chosen field. By understanding our natural talents, we can seek out roles and opportunities that allow us to leverage those strengths, leading to greater job satisfaction and performance.

In addition to professional pursuits, knowing our strengths is valuable in personal relationships. It enables us to foster connections with others who appreciate and complement our strengths, leading to more harmonious and fulfilling relationships. When we understand our strengths, we can also communicate them effectively, allowing others to recognize and appreciate our contributions.

Identifying our strengths also enhances our self-confidence and self-esteem. When we are aware of our unique abilities and recognize the value they bring, we develop a positive self-perception. This self-assurance allows us to tackle challenges with a greater sense of belief in our capabilities, leading to increased resilience and a willingness to step outside our comfort zone.

Furthermore, understanding our strengths helps us prioritize our time and energy. By focusing on activities that align with our strengths, we can optimize our productivity and effectiveness. Instead of spreading ourselves too thin trying to improve in areas where we may have limited potential, we can channel our resources towards activities that capitalize on our strengths, leading to greater efficiency and overall success.

It's important to note that strengths are not fixed traits. They can evolve and develop over time through intentional effort and practice. By continuously investing in our strengths and seeking opportunities for growth, we can further expand our capabilities and reach new levels of proficiency.

Finally, the process of identifying strengths is a journey of self-discovery and self-awareness. It requires reflection, exploration, and a willingness to embrace our authentic selves. It may involve taking risks and stepping outside our comfort zone to truly understand and unleash our full potential.

In conclusion, identifying and leveraging our strengths and talents is a powerful tool for personal and professional growth. By recognizing our unique qualities, we can harness our natural abilities, pursue opportunities that align with our strengths, and cultivate a fulfilling and successful life. When we operate from a place of strength, we not only enhance our own well-being but also contribute positively to the world around us. So take the time to identify your strengths, embrace them, and let them guide you towards a life of purpose and achievement.

Chapter 22: The art of effective time management.

Time is a valuable resource, and how we manage it can greatly impact our productivity, success, and overall well-being. In this chapter, we explore the art of effective time management and provide practical strategies to optimize our use of time, prioritize tasks, and achieve our goals.

Effective time management is about making conscious choices and taking control of how we allocate our time. It involves setting goals, organizing our tasks, and utilizing strategies to maximize productivity and efficiency. By managing our time effectively, we can reduce stress, increase productivity, and create a greater sense of balance in our lives.

The first step in effective time management is setting clear goals. Goals provide a sense of direction and purpose, guiding our actions and decisions. By defining our objectives, both short-term and long-term, we can prioritize our tasks and allocate our time accordingly. Setting SMART goals (specific, measurable, achievable, relevant, time-bound) helps ensure that our goals are clear, realistic, and actionable.

Once goals are established, it's important to create a system for organizing tasks and activities. This can be done through various tools and techniques, such as to-do lists, calendars, or digital productivity apps. Breaking down large tasks into smaller, manageable steps can help prevent overwhelm and make progress more achievable. Prioritizing tasks based on urgency, importance, and alignment with our goals allows us to focus our time and energy on what truly matters.

One effective time management technique is the "pomodoro technique," which involves working in focused intervals followed by short breaks. This method helps maintain concentration and prevents burnout. By dividing our work into 25-minute intervals (known as "pomodoros") and taking short breaks in between, we can enhance productivity and maintain mental freshness.

Another important aspect of effective time management is learning to delegate and say no. Recognizing that we can't do everything ourselves and being comfortable delegating tasks to others allows us to free up time for higher-priority responsibilities. Additionally, learning to say no to non-essential commitments or activities that don't align with our goals helps us protect our time and focus on what truly matters.

Managing distractions is crucial in optimizing our use of time. In today's digital age, distractions are plentiful, from social media notifications to email overload. Implementing strategies such as setting designated times for checking emails, turning off notifications during focused work periods, or utilizing website-blocking apps can help minimize distractions and maintain focus.

Furthermore, effective time management involves balancing productivity with self-care. Taking regular breaks, engaging in physical activity, and practicing mindfulness or relaxation techniques can rejuvenate our energy and improve overall productivity. It's important to recognize that rest and rejuvenation are not time wasted but essential for maintaining a sustainable level of productivity.

Effective time management also includes the ability to adapt and be flexible. Priorities and circumstances can change, and it's important to be agile in adjusting our plans and schedules accordingly. Being able to assess and reassess our priorities allows us to make informed decisions and adapt to new challenges or opportunities that arise.

Finally, it's crucial to regularly evaluate and reflect on our time management practices. Assessing what is working well and what needs improvement allows us to refine our strategies and continually optimize our use of time. Being mindful of time-wasting habits, such as excessive multitasking or procrastination, empowers us to make positive changes and cultivate more productive habits.

In conclusion, effective time management is a skill that can significantly enhance our productivity, reduce stress, and improve our overall quality of life. By setting clear goals, organizing tasks, managing distractions, and prioritizing self-care, we can optimize our use of time and achieve our desired outcomes. Remember, time is a limited resource, and how we choose to utilize it ultimately shapes

Chapter 23: Boosting productivity and focus.

―――

In today's fast-paced world, staying productive and maintaining focus are crucial for achieving our goals and making the most of our time. In this chapter, we delve into strategies and techniques to boost productivity and enhance our ability to concentrate on tasks effectively.

1.Clear goals and priorities: Clearly defined goals provide a sense of direction and purpose. When we have a clear vision of what we want to accomplish, it becomes easier to prioritize tasks and allocate our time accordingly. Break down large goals into smaller, actionable steps, and establish priorities based on urgency and importance.

2.Time blocking: Time blocking involves scheduling specific time blocks for different activities or tasks. By assigning dedicated time slots for focused work, meetings, breaks, and personal activities, we create structure and ensure that essential tasks receive the necessary attention. This technique helps minimize distractions and promotes better time management.

3.Task prioritization: Prioritizing tasks is essential for maximizing productivity. Identify the most important and high-impact tasks and tackle them first. The Eisenhower Matrix, which categorizes tasks based on their urgency and importance, can be a useful tool for prioritization. Focus your energy on tasks that align with your goals and contribute to long-term success.

4.Single-tasking: Multitasking can be tempting, but it often leads to decreased productivity and reduced quality of work. Instead, practice single-tasking, which involves focusing on one task at a time until completion or a designated break. This allows for better concentration and a more thorough and efficient approach to tasks.

5.Minimize distractions: Distractions can derail productivity and disrupt focus. Identify common distractions in your environment, such as social media notifications, email alerts, or noise, and take steps to minimize or eliminate them. Consider using website-blocking apps, turning off non-essential notifications, or designating specific times for checking emails to maintain focus.

6.Time management techniques: Explore different time management techniques to find what works best for you. Some popular techniques include the Pomodoro Technique, where work is divided into focused intervals with short breaks, and the 80/20 rule, which suggests that 80% of our results come from 20% of our efforts. Experiment with various techniques to discover which ones optimize your productivity and focus.

7.Create a productive environment: Your physical environment plays a significant role in your productivity and focus. Ensure that your workspace is clean, organized, and free from clutter. Personalize it with items that inspire and motivate you. Consider incorporating elements that promote focus, such as good lighting, comfortable furniture, and noise-canceling headphones.

8.Optimize energy levels: Productivity and focus are closely tied to our energy levels. Take care of your physical and mental well-being by getting sufficient sleep, eating nutritious meals, and staying hydrated. Regular exercise, breaks for stretching or walking, and mindfulness practices can also boost energy levels and enhance focus.

9.Eliminate procrastination: Procrastination can be a productivity killer. Identify the root causes of your procrastination tendencies and implement strategies to overcome them. Break tasks into smaller, more manageable steps, set deadlines, and hold yourself accountable. Use techniques like the "5-second rule" (where you take action within five seconds of having an idea) to combat procrastination and cultivate a proactive mindset.

10.Continuous learning and skill development: Invest in ongoing learning and skill development to enhance your productivity and focus. Stay up-to-date with industry trends, acquire new knowledge, and develop relevant skills. This not only increases your value but also keeps you engaged and motivated in your work.

Remember, productivity and focus are habits that require consistent practice and dedication. It's essential to find a balance that works for you and adapt strategies to fit

your individual needs and preferences. Here are a few additional tips to further boost your productivity and focus:

11.Break tasks into smaller chunks: Large projects or tasks can be overwhelming and lead to procrastination. Break them down into smaller, more manageable parts. This not only makes them less intimidating but also provides a clear roadmap for completion.

12.Utilize technology tools: Take advantage of technology tools and apps designed to enhance productivity and focus. From project management software to task-tracking apps and digital calendars, there are numerous tools available to help you stay organized, manage your time effectively, and stay on track.

13.Practice mindfulness and meditation: Incorporate mindfulness and meditation practices into your daily routine. These techniques can help improve focus, reduce stress, and increase mental clarity. Set aside a few minutes each day to engage in deep breathing exercises or guided meditation to enhance your overall productivity.

14.Avoid multitasking: While multitasking may seem like a way to accomplish more in less time, it actually hinders productivity and focus. Instead, focus on one task at a time and give it your full attention. By immersing yourself in a single task, you can achieve better results in less time.

15.Take regular breaks: Breaks are essential for maintaining productivity and preventing burnout. Incorporate short breaks into your work schedule to recharge and refresh your mind. Use this time to engage in activities that relax and rejuvenate you, such as taking a walk, practicing a hobby, or simply resting.

16.Set realistic deadlines: Establish realistic deadlines for your tasks and projects. Avoid overcommitting yourself and creating unnecessary pressure. By setting achievable deadlines, you can maintain focus, reduce stress, and deliver high-quality work.

17.Delegate when possible: Recognize when tasks can be delegated to others. Delegating not only frees up your time but also allows you to focus on higher-value tasks. Trust your team members or colleagues to handle certain responsibilities, and use your time and energy where they are most needed.

18.Practice effective communication: Clear and effective communication is key to productivity and focus. Ensure that you have a clear understanding of tasks and expectations, and communicate openly with colleagues or team members. Regularly provide updates on your progress and ask for clarification when needed.

19.Embrace a growth mindset: Adopting a growth mindset encourages continuous learning and improvement. Embrace challenges as opportunities for growth and view setbacks as learning experiences. This mindset helps you stay motivated, resilient, and focused on long-term goals.

20.Celebrate achievements: Acknowledge and celebrate your accomplishments along the way. Recognizing your progress and achievements boosts motivation and enhances your overall sense of satisfaction. Take time to reflect on your successes and use them as fuel to drive further productivity and focus.

By implementing these strategies and incorporating them into your daily routine, you can significantly boost your productivity and focus. Remember, productivity is not about working longer hours but rather about working smarter and utilizing your time effectively. With dedication, practice, and a commitment to personal growth, you can achieve your goals and lead a fulfilling and successful life.

Chapter 24: Creativity and problem-solving skills.

———

C reativity and problem-solving skills are essential in today's rapidly changing world. In this chapter, we explore the importance of fostering creativity and developing effective problem-solving abilities. By embracing these skills, we can find innovative solutions, overcome challenges, and unlock new opportunities.

1.Understanding creativity: Creativity is not limited to artists or musicians; it is a fundamental human trait that can be nurtured and developed. It involves thinking outside the box, making connections between seemingly unrelated ideas, and approaching problems with an open mind. Recognize that everyone has the potential to be creative in their own unique way.

2.Embracing a growth mindset: Adopting a growth mindset is crucial for enhancing creativity and problem-solving skills. Embrace challenges as opportunities for growth and view failures as learning experiences. Believe that you can develop and improve your creative abilities with effort and practice.

3.Cultivating curiosity: Curiosity fuels creativity. Stay curious and constantly seek new knowledge and experiences. Ask questions, explore different perspectives, and challenge assumptions. Engage in activities that stimulate your curiosity, such as reading diverse books, attending lectures or workshops, or engaging in hobbies outside your comfort zone.

4.Divergent thinking: Divergent thinking is a key component of creativity. It involves generating multiple ideas and exploring different possibilities. Practice brainstorming techniques, such as mind mapping or free writing, to stimulate divergent thinking and expand your creative problem-solving abilities.

5.Enhancing flexibility and adaptability: Creativity thrives in an environment of flexibility and adaptability. Embrace change and be open to new ideas and perspectives. Be willing to modify your approach, experiment with different solutions, and adapt to unexpected circumstances.

6.Creating an inspiring environment: Your physical and mental environment can significantly impact your creativity. Surround yourself with inspiration by curating a space that encourages creative thinking. Include elements like artwork, books, or motivational quotes that resonate with your interests and passions.

7.Encourage collaboration and feedback: Collaboration with others can spark creativity and enhance problem-solving skills. Engage in brainstorming sessions or seek input from diverse perspectives. Welcome constructive feedback and consider alternative viewpoints, as they can lead to breakthrough ideas and solutions.

8.Embrace risk-taking: Creativity often involves taking risks and stepping outside your comfort zone. Don't be afraid of failure or making mistakes. See them as valuable learning opportunities and stepping stones to creative growth. Embrace experimentation and be willing to explore unconventional approaches.

9.Break patterns and routines: Breaking free from patterns and routines can ignite creativity. Challenge yourself to break established habits and try new approaches. Explore different methodologies, techniques, or tools that can stimulate fresh thinking and problem-solving.

10.Continuous learning: Learning is a lifelong process that fuels creativity and problem-solving. Stay curious and continuously expand your knowledge base. Explore new subjects, acquire diverse skills, and stay updated on the latest trends and innovations in your field. The more you know, the more diverse the range of ideas and solutions you can draw upon.

11.Practice mindfulness and reflection: Mindfulness and reflection can help quiet the mind, enhance focus, and stimulate creative thinking. Set aside regular time for mindfulness practices, such as meditation or journaling, to tap into your inner creativity. Reflect on your experiences, challenges, and successes, and use them as inspiration for future creative endeavors.

12.Overcoming mental blocks: Creativity can sometimes be hindered by mental blocks. Recognize and address common barriers like self-doubt, fear of judgment, or perfectionism. Cultivate a positive mindset, practice self-compassion, and embrace a "fail forward" mentality to overcome these obstacles and unleash your creative potential.

13.Embrace serendipity: Serendipity refers to unexpected discoveries or fortunate coincidences that can spark creativity. Embrace serendipity by remaining open to new experiences and opportunities. Engage in diverse activities, connect with different people, and expose yourself to new environments. Sometimes, the most creative ideas arise from unexpected encounters or chance encounters.

14.Use creative thinking techniques: There are various creative thinking techniques that can enhance your problem-solving skills. These include brainstorming, mind mapping, lateral thinking, and the SCAMPER technique (Substitute, Combine, Adapt, Modify, Put to another use, Eliminate, Rearrange). Experiment with different techniques to stimulate your creative thinking and generate innovative solutions.

15.Take breaks and seek inspiration: Creativity requires mental rejuvenation. Take regular breaks to recharge your mind and seek inspiration from various sources. Explore art, music, nature, or engaging in hobbies that inspire you. These moments of relaxation and inspiration can spark new ideas and perspectives.

16.Embrace failure as a learning opportunity: Failure is an inherent part of the creative process. Embrace it as a valuable learning opportunity rather than a setback. Analyze the lessons learned from failure, adjust your approach, and apply newfound knowledge to future endeavors. Remember, some of the most successful innovations have emerged from initial failures.

17.Foster a positive and supportive environment: Surround yourself with individuals who support and encourage your creativity. Seek out like-minded individuals who appreciate and value creative thinking. Engage in constructive discussions and collaborations that nurture and amplify your creative ideas.

18.Practice creative problem-solving: Creative problem-solving involves identifying unique solutions to challenges. Break down complex problems into manageable parts, approach them from different angles, and consider unconventional perspectives. Combine your creative thinking skills with analytical reasoning to find effective and innovative solutions.

19.Embrace simplicity: Sometimes, the most creative solutions are the simplest ones. Avoid overcomplicating problems and focus on finding elegant and straightforward solutions. Look for simplicity in design, processes, and communication to enhance clarity and effectiveness.

20.Cultivate a creative routine: Establish a creative routine that allows you to regularly engage in activities that stimulate your creativity. Dedicate specific time slots each day or week for creative endeavors such as brainstorming, sketching, or experimenting. Consistency and regular practice can enhance your creative thinking abilities over time.

By embracing creativity and developing effective problem-solving skills, you can navigate challenges with confidence and uncover innovative solutions. Remember, creativity is a skill that can be honed with practice and a willingness to think outside the box. Embrace curiosity, stay open-minded, and persist in the face of obstacles. With these qualities, you can tap into your creative potential and bring fresh perspectives and solutions to any situation.

Chapter 25: Dealing with professional challenges.

———

In the fast-paced and competitive professional world, it's inevitable to face various challenges along the way. This chapter explores strategies and techniques for effectively dealing with professional challenges and overcoming obstacles that may arise in your career journey.

1.Embrace a growth mindset: Adopting a growth mindset is essential when facing professional challenges. See obstacles as opportunities for growth and development. Believe that with effort, perseverance, and a positive attitude, you can overcome any challenge and continue to learn and improve.

2.Develop resilience: Resilience is the ability to bounce back from setbacks and adapt to change. Cultivate resilience by building a strong support network, practicing self-care, and developing effective coping mechanisms. Maintain a positive outlook and use challenges as stepping stones for personal and professional growth.

3.Seek feedback and learning opportunities: Feedback is a valuable tool for growth and improvement. Seek feedback from colleagues, mentors, or supervisors to gain insights into your strengths and areas for development. Actively pursue learning opportunities, such as attending workshops or conferences, taking courses, or participating in professional development programs.

4.Develop problem-solving skills: Effective problem-solving skills are crucial for overcoming professional challenges. Break down complex problems into smaller, manageable tasks. Analyze the situation, explore potential solutions, and evaluate the pros and cons of each option. Utilize critical thinking and creativity to find innovative solutions to challenges.

5.Build a supportive network: Surround yourself with a supportive network of colleagues, mentors, and like-minded professionals. Share your challenges and seek advice and guidance from those who have faced similar situations. Collaborate with others to brainstorm solutions and leverage their expertise and perspectives.

6.Manage stress and maintain work-life balance: Professional challenges can be stressful and impact your overall well-being. Practice stress management techniques such as exercise, mindfulness, and prioritizing self-care. Maintain a healthy work-life balance to prevent burnout and ensure you have the energy and focus to tackle challenges effectively.

7.Develop effective communication skills: Communication is key when dealing with professional challenges. Clearly articulate your thoughts and concerns, actively listen to others, and seek to understand different perspectives. Effective communication fosters collaboration, problem-solving, and finding mutually beneficial solutions.

8.Set realistic expectations: It's important to set realistic expectations for yourself and others. Understand your limitations and prioritize tasks based on their importance and urgency. Communicate openly about timelines, deliverables, and potential challenges to manage expectations effectively.

9.Continuously learn and adapt: The professional landscape is ever-evolving, and continuous learning is crucial for success. Stay updated with industry trends, technological advancements, and best practices in your field. Adapt to changes and be proactive in seeking new skills and knowledge to stay ahead of the curve.

10.Embrace change and adaptability: Change is inevitable in any professional setting. Embrace it as an opportunity for growth and adaptation. Develop the ability to quickly adjust to new circumstances, acquire new skills, and embrace different approaches. Those who can adapt to change are more likely to overcome challenges and thrive in their careers.

11.Cultivate a positive mindset: Maintaining a positive mindset is essential when facing professional challenges. Focus on solutions rather than dwelling on problems. Celebrate successes, no matter how small, and use them as motivation to persevere through challenges. Surround yourself with positive influences and engage in activities that uplift your spirits.

12.Develop time management skills: Effective time management is crucial for navigating professional challenges. Prioritize tasks, set realistic deadlines, and allocate your time and energy efficiently. Use productivity tools and techniques to stay organized and focused, minimizing stress and maximizing your productivity.

13.Seek opportunities for growth: View professional challenges as opportunities for growth and skill development. Volunteer for challenging projects, take on additional responsibilities, and seek out opportunities to stretch your skills and knowledge. Embrace new assignments or roles that push you outside your comfort zone. By actively seeking growth opportunities, you can turn professional challenges into stepping stones for advancement.

14.Develop emotional intelligence: Emotional intelligence is the ability to recognize and manage emotions, both in yourself and others. It plays a significant role in navigating professional challenges. Develop self-awareness to understand your own emotions and reactions to challenging situations. Practice empathy to understand the perspectives and emotions of others involved. Use emotional intelligence to navigate conflicts, build strong relationships, and find collaborative solutions.

15.Stay persistent and resilient: Professional challenges often require persistence and resilience to overcome. Maintain a strong belief in yourself and your abilities, even in the face of setbacks. Be persistent in your efforts, continuously seeking solutions and alternative approaches. Learn from failures and use them as fuel for future success.

16.Seek support from mentors: Mentors can provide invaluable guidance and support when facing professional challenges. Identify mentors who have experienced similar challenges or have expertise in the areas you're struggling with. Seek their advice, share your concerns, and learn from their experiences. Their insights and encouragement can help you navigate difficult situations with more confidence and clarity.

17.Take ownership of your development: Ultimately, you are responsible for your professional growth and development. Take ownership of your career path by setting goals, seeking out learning opportunities, and continuously assessing your progress. Regularly reflect on your strengths and areas for improvement, and take proactive steps to enhance your skills and knowledge.

18.Celebrate milestones and successes: As you overcome professional challenges, take the time to acknowledge and celebrate your achievements. Recognize the progress you've made, no matter how small. Celebrating milestones and successes boosts your confidence, reinforces positive behaviors, and motivates you to tackle future challenges.

19.Foster a positive supportive environment: Surround yourself with colleagues and organizations that foster a positive and supportive environment. Seek out workplaces that encourage collaboration, provide resources for growth and development, and value employee well-being. A supportive environment can provide the necessary encouragement and resources to overcome professional challenges.

20.Learn from past experiences: Reflect on past professional challenges and the strategies you used to overcome them. Identify patterns and lessons learned that can be applied to current and future situations. By drawing from your past experiences, you can develop a repertoire of effective approaches to tackle new challenges.

Dealing with professional challenges requires a combination of resilience, adaptability, effective communication, and a growth mindset. By incorporating these strategies into your professional journey, you can navigate obstacles with confidence and turn challenges into opportunities for growth and success. Remember, each challenge is a chance to learn, develop new skills, and emerge stronger on the other side.

Chapter 26: The basics of financial education.

———

F inancial literacy is a critical skill that empowers individuals to make informed decisions about their money and achieve financial well-being. In this chapter, we will explore the basics of financial education and equip you with essential knowledge and skills to manage your finances effectively.

1.Understanding personal finance: Start by gaining a clear understanding of personal finance concepts. Learn about budgeting, saving, investing, debt management, and retirement planning. Familiarize yourself with financial terms and concepts to make informed decisions about your money.

2.Setting financial goals: Identify your short-term and long-term financial goals. Whether it's buying a house, saving for education, or building an emergency fund, setting specific and measurable goals provides direction and motivation for your financial journey.

3.Creating a budget: A budget is a fundamental tool for managing your finances. Track your income and expenses to understand where your money is going. Allocate your income wisely, ensuring you prioritize essential expenses while also saving and investing for the future.

4.Managing debt: Understand different types of debt and their implications. Learn strategies to manage and reduce debt effectively. Make a plan to pay off high-interest debts first and avoid unnecessary borrowing whenever possible.

5. Saving and investing: Develop a savings habit to build a financial cushion for unexpected expenses and future goals. Learn about different savings vehicles, such as savings accounts, certificates of deposit, and money market accounts. Explore investment options, including stocks, bonds, mutual funds, and real estate, to grow your wealth over time.

6. Understanding credit: Familiarize yourself with credit scores, credit reports, and the factors that influence them. Learn how to establish and maintain good credit. Understand the importance of responsible credit card usage and the impact of credit on your financial well-being.

7. Insurance and risk management: Gain knowledge about insurance options, such as health insurance, life insurance, and property insurance. Understand the importance of protecting yourself and your assets against unexpected events and emergencies.

8. Retirement planning: Start planning for your retirement early in your career. Learn about retirement accounts, such as 401(k)s and individual retirement accounts (IRAs). Understand the power of compounding and the benefits of contributing to retirement savings consistently.

9. Tax basics: Familiarize yourself with the basics of income taxes. Understand different tax deductions and credits that may apply to you. Seek professional advice or use tax

software to ensure compliance with tax laws and maximize your tax savings.

10. Financial risk management: Evaluate and manage financial risks effectively. Understand the importance of diversification and asset allocation in investment portfolios. Consider your risk tolerance and time horizon when making investment decisions.

11. Estate planning: Learn about estate planning and the importance of having a will, power of attorney, and healthcare directive. Understand how to protect your assets and ensure they are distributed according to your wishes.

12. Financial education resources: Take advantage of various resources available to enhance your financial education. Attend workshops, seminars, or webinars offered by financial institutions, community organizations, or online platforms. Read books, articles, and blogs written by financial experts. Consider taking courses or pursuing certifications in financial planning or investment management.

13. Seek professional advice: When necessary, seek the assistance of financial professionals, such as financial advisors, tax experts, or estate planners. They can provide personalized guidance and help you make informed financial decisions based on your specific circumstances.

14. Continuous learning: Financial education is an ongoing process. Stay updated with changes in financial markets, tax laws, and personal finance trends. Stay curious and continue learning to adapt to evolving financial landscapes.

By understanding the basics of personal finance and developing financial literacy, you can take control of your financial future. Educate yourself, set financial goals, and make informed decisions about budgeting, saving, investing, and managing debt. With a solid foundation in financial education, you can navigate the complexities of the financial world and make choices that align with your long-term financial goals.

15. Avoiding financial pitfalls: Financial education also involves being aware of common financial pitfalls and taking steps to avoid them. Learn about the dangers of predatory lending, high-interest loans, and scams targeting unsuspecting individuals. Develop the skills to critically evaluate financial products and make sound decisions that protect your financial well-being.

16. Building an emergency fund: An emergency fund is an essential component of financial stability. Learn how to establish an emergency fund that covers three to six months' worth of living expenses. This fund acts as a safety net during unexpected events, such as job loss or medical emergencies, preventing you from relying on credit or depleting your savings.

17. Understanding investment options: Explore various investment options and understand the associated risks and potential returns. Learn about stocks, bonds, mutual funds, exchange-traded funds (ETFs), and other investment vehicles. Consider your risk tolerance, investment goals, and time horizon when creating an investment portfolio that aligns with your financial objectives.

18.Making informed spending decisions: Financial education empowers you to make informed spending decisions. Learn how to differentiate between needs and wants, prioritize essential expenses, and practice mindful spending. Develop strategies to avoid impulsive purchases and cultivate healthy financial habits.

19.Monitoring and reviewing your finances: Regularly monitor and review your financial situation to ensure you stay on track with your goals. Review your budget, track your expenses, and assess your progress towards achieving financial milestones. This ongoing evaluation allows you to make necessary adjustments and stay proactive in managing your finances.

20.Teaching financial literacy to others: Share your knowledge and help others improve their financial literacy. Educate family members, friends, or community members about the importance of financial education and provide them with resources and guidance to enhance their financial well-being. By spreading financial literacy, you contribute to building a financially empowered society.

21.Planning for major life events: Financial education prepares you for major life events that have financial implications. Whether it's buying a home, getting married, having children, or starting a business, understanding the financial aspects of these milestones helps you make informed decisions and mitigate potential risks.

22.Balancing short-term and long-term financial goals: Financial education teaches you to strike a balance between short-term and long-term financial goals. While it's important to enjoy the present, planning for the future is equally crucial. Learn strategies to allocate your resources effectively, ensuring you meet your immediate needs while also saving and investing for long-term financial security.

23.Evaluating financial products and services: When choosing financial products and services, such as bank accounts, credit cards, or insurance policies, financial education allows you to evaluate their features, fees, and benefits. Understand the terms and conditions, compare different options, and make informed decisions that align with your financial goals and values.

24.Understanding economic trends: Stay informed about economic trends and their potential impact on your finances. Learn about inflation, interest rates, and market fluctuations. This knowledge enables you to make strategic financial decisions, such as adjusting your investment portfolio or planning for potential economic downturns.

25.Cultivating financial confidence: Financial education instills confidence in your ability to manage your money effectively. As you gain knowledge and develop practical skills, your confidence grows, allowing you to navigate financial challenges with resilience and make decisions that align with your values and goals.

26.Implementing sustainable financial practices: Financial education promotes sustainable financial practices. Learn about sustainable investing, responsible consumption, and ethical financial choices. Understand how your financial decisions can have social and environmental impacts, and make choices that align with your values.

By embracing the basics of financial education, you gain the knowledge and skills necessary to take control of your financial future. With a solid understanding of personal finance, you can make informed decisions, avoid common pitfalls, and work towards achieving your financial goals.

27.Building wealth: Financial education empowers you to build wealth over time. Learn about strategies such as investing in appreciating assets, diversifying your portfolio, and leveraging compound interest. By adopting a long-term perspective and making smart financial choices, you can accumulate wealth and create a solid foundation for your future.

28.Understanding taxes: Taxes are a significant part of personal finance. Educate yourself about tax laws and regulations in your jurisdiction. Learn about deductions, credits, and tax-efficient strategies to minimize your tax liability and maximize your financial resources.

29.Planning for retirement: Retirement planning is crucial for long-term financial security. Learn about different retirement accounts, such as 401(k)s, IRAs, and pension plans. Understand the importance of starting early, contributing consistently, and regularly reviewing your retirement plan to ensure you're on track to meet your retirement goals.

30.Estate planning: Estate planning involves organizing your assets and making decisions about their distribution after your passing. Learn about wills, trusts, powers of attorney, and healthcare directives. Understand how estate taxes and probate laws may affect your estate. By engaging in proper estate planning, you can protect your assets and ensure your wishes are carried out.

31.Entrepreneurship and business finances: If you aspire to start your own business, financial education is essential. Learn about business finances, cash flow management, budgeting for startups, and securing financing. Understand the financial risks and rewards of entrepreneurship and develop the financial skills needed to run a successful business.

32.Financial well-being and happiness: Financial education goes beyond money management; it also contributes to your overall well-being and happiness. Understand the link between financial stress and mental health. Learn strategies to reduce financial stress, cultivate a healthy relationship with money, and align your financial choices with your values and life goals.

33.Adapting to economic changes: Economic landscapes are ever-changing. Financial education equips you with the knowledge to adapt to economic shifts and make informed decisions. Stay informed about market trends, economic indicators, and emerging industries. By understanding economic changes, you can position yourself for financial success in different economic conditions.

34.Insurance and risk management: Learn about different insurance types, such as health insurance, auto insurance, and homeowner's insurance. Understand the importance of insurance in protecting your financial well-being against unexpected events, accidents, or liability claims. Assess your insurance needs and make informed choices to mitigate financial risks.

35.Philanthropy and giving: Financial education can also inspire a sense of social responsibility and philanthropy. Understand the impact of charitable giving and explore ways to incorporate giving into your financial plan. Whether through donations, volunteering, or supporting causes you care about, financial education can help you make a positive difference in your community.

36.Financial ethics and responsibility: Financial education emphasizes the importance of ethical behavior and responsible financial practices. Learn about financial regulations, consumer rights, and ethical investing. Make choices that align with your values and contribute to a more sustainable and equitable financial system.

37.Lifelong learning: Financial education is a lifelong journey. Stay curious and continue to expand your knowledge and skills in personal finance. Attend seminars, webinars, and workshops. Read books, articles, and blogs by financial experts. Engage in discussions and seek advice from professionals. By committing to continuous learning, you can stay ahead in an ever-evolving financial landscape.

In conclusion, Chapter 26 of your self-help book introduces the basics of financial education. By embracing financial literacy, you gain the knowledge and skills necessary to manage your money effectively, make informed decisions, and work towards achieving your financial goals. Financial education also empowers you to navigate the complexities of the financial world, protect yourself from financial pitfalls, and adapt to economic changes. It helps you build wealth, plan for retirement, and make wise investment decisions. Additionally, financial education encompasses important aspects such as taxes, estate planning, entrepreneurship, and risk management.

One of the key benefits of financial education is the ability to cultivate financial well-being and happiness. By understanding the relationship between financial stress and mental health, you can adopt strategies to reduce financial stress and establish a healthy relationship with money. This includes aligning your financial choices with your values and life goals, practicing mindful spending, and finding a balance between present enjoyment and future financial security.

Moreover, financial education equips you with the skills to adapt to economic changes. Economic landscapes are dynamic, and staying informed about market trends and emerging industries allows you to make informed decisions and seize opportunities. By understanding economic shifts and adapting your financial strategies accordingly, you can position yourself for long-term financial success.

Insurance and risk management are also crucial components of financial education. Understanding different types of insurance and their role in protecting your financial well-being is essential. By assessing your insurance needs and making informed choices, you can mitigate financial risks and safeguard your assets against unexpected events.

Furthermore, financial education can inspire a sense of social responsibility and philanthropy. Understanding the impact of charitable giving and incorporating giving into your financial plan allows you to make a positive difference in your community. By aligning your financial choices with your values and supporting causes you care about, you contribute to creating a more equitable and sustainable society.

Ethics and responsibility are integral aspects of financial education. By familiarizing yourself with financial regulations, consumer rights, and ethical investing, you can make choices that align with your values and contribute to a more responsible and equitable financial system. This includes being mindful of the environmental and social impacts of your financial decisions and seeking investments that prioritize sustainability and social good.

Lastly, financial education is a lifelong journey. Committing to continuous learning and staying updated with the latest financial trends and strategies ensures that you remain knowledgeable and adaptable in the ever-changing financial landscape. Engaging in ongoing education through seminars, workshops, reading, and seeking professional advice enables you to make informed decisions and continuously improve your financial well-being.

In summary, Chapter 26 of your self-help book highlights the importance of financial education. It emphasizes the value of understanding personal finance, setting financial goals, and making informed decisions about budgeting, saving, investing, and debt management. Financial education empowers you to build wealth, plan for retirement, navigate economic changes, and cultivate financial well-being. By incorporating the principles of financial education into your life, you can take control of your financial future and work towards achieving long-term financial security and happiness.

Chapter 27: Budgeting and saving.

Introduction:

Budgeting and saving are fundamental aspects of personal finance. They lay the foundation for financial stability and success, allowing you to manage your income effectively, prioritize your expenses, and work towards achieving your financial goals. In this chapter, we will explore the importance of budgeting, learn how to create a budget, and discover effective strategies for saving money.

The importance of budgeting:

1.Budgeting is the process of creating a plan for your income and expenses. It provides a clear picture of where your money is coming from and where it is going. Budgeting helps you:

● Gain control: By tracking your income and expenses, you gain control over your financial situation. It allows you to make intentional decisions about how you allocate your resources.

● Identify spending habits: Budgeting helps you identify areas where you may be overspending or wasting money. It allows you to recognize patterns and make adjustments to align your spending with your financial goals.

● Prioritize your expenses: A budget helps you prioritize your expenses based on your values and financial objectives. It ensures that you allocate money towards the things that matter most to you.

Creating a budget:

2.Creating a budget involves several steps:

- Track your income: Begin by identifying all sources of income, including your salary, investments, and any additional income streams. Calculate your total monthly income.

- List your expenses: Make a comprehensive list of all your expenses, including fixed expenses (rent/mortgage, utilities, insurance), variable expenses (groceries, transportation, entertainment), and discretionary expenses (eating out, shopping). Be thorough and include even the smallest expenses.

- Categorize your expenses: Group your expenses into categories to gain a better understanding of your spending patterns. This allows you to identify areas where you can potentially reduce expenses.

- Set financial goals: Determine your financial goals, such as saving for emergencies, paying off debt, or saving for a down payment on a home. Allocate a portion of your income towards these goals.

- Allocate your income: Based on your income and expenses, allocate a specific amount for each category. Be realistic and ensure that your income covers all essential expenses while leaving room for savings.

- Monitor and adjust: Regularly monitor your budget and make adjustments as needed. Life circumstances and financial goals may change, requiring you to revise your budget accordingly.

Effective saving strategies:

3.In addition to budgeting, saving money is crucial for long-term financial security. Here are some effective saving strategies to consider:

• Pay yourself first: Make saving a priority by automating your savings. Set up automatic transfers from your checking account to a separate savings account or retirement account. Treat your savings like a bill that must be paid.

• Start an emergency fund: Build an emergency fund to cover unexpected expenses, such as medical bills or car repairs. Aim to save three to six months' worth of living expenses. Start small and gradually increase your savings over time.

• Reduce discretionary expenses: Analyze your discretionary expenses and look for areas where you can cut back. Consider reducing eating out, entertainment, or unnecessary subscriptions. Redirect the money saved towards your savings goals.

• Set short-term and long-term savings goals: Identify short-term and long-term savings goals, such as a vacation, a new car, or retirement. Set specific targets and create a timeline for achieving them. Having clear goals provides motivation and focus.

• Minimize debt: High-interest debt can hinder your ability to save. Develop a plan to pay off your debts systematically.

Focus on paying off high-interest debts first while making minimum payments on others.

• Explore saving options: Research different saving options, such as high-yield savings accounts or investment vehicles like individual retirement accounts (IRAs) or employer-sponsored retirement plans. Understand the risks and potential returns associated with each option before making a decision.

• Automate savings: Make saving effortless by automating your savings. Set up automatic transfers from your checking account to your savings account on a regular basis. This eliminates the temptation to spend the money and ensures consistent saving.

• Track your progress: Regularly track your savings progress to stay motivated and accountable. Monitor your savings account balance, review your budget, and celebrate milestones along the way. Seeing your savings grow can provide a sense of accomplishment and encourage you to continue saving.

• Seek ways to increase income: Consider ways to increase your income to boost your savings. This could involve negotiating a raise or promotion at work, starting a side business or freelance gig, or finding additional sources of income. The extra money can be allocated towards savings.

• Involve the whole family: If you have a family, involve everyone in the budgeting and saving process. Teach children about the importance of money management and involve them in setting family financial goals. Encourage open communication about money and work together as a team.

- Stay disciplined: Saving requires discipline and commitment. Stay focused on your financial goals and resist the temptation to deviate from your budget. Remind yourself of the long-term benefits of saving and the financial security it brings.

- Continuously educate yourself: Stay informed about personal finance and savings strategies. Read books, attend seminars, and follow reputable financial experts to enhance your knowledge. The more you learn, the better equipped you'll be to make sound financial decisions.

Conclusion:

Chapter 27 highlights the significance of budgeting and saving in achieving financial stability and reaching your financial goals. By creating a budget, you gain control over your finances, prioritize expenses, and make informed decisions. Implementing effective saving strategies allows you to build an emergency fund, reduce debt, and work towards short-term and long-term savings goals. Remember, budgeting and saving are ongoing practices that require discipline and commitment. By adopting these habits, you can establish a solid financial foundation and pave the way for a secure and prosperous future.

Chapter 28: Debt reduction and wealth building.

———

I ntroduction:

Debt can be a significant obstacle on the path to financial freedom and wealth accumulation. In Chapter 28, we will explore the importance of debt reduction and effective strategies for building wealth. By understanding how to manage and reduce debt, you can take control of your financial future and pave the way for long-term wealth creation.

Understanding debt:

1.Debt comes in various forms, such as credit card debt, student loans, mortgages, and car loans. While some forms of debt may be necessary, excessive debt can hinder your financial progress. It is essential to understand the different types of debt, their associated interest rates, and repayment terms.

The impact of debt on financial health:

2.Carrying high levels of debt can have several negative consequences, including:

● High interest payments: Debt often comes with interest charges, which can add up over time. High-interest rates can make it challenging to pay off the principal amount, resulting in a cycle of debt.

• Limited cash flow: Debt payments can consume a significant portion of your monthly income, limiting your ability to save, invest, and build wealth.

• Credit score and borrowing capacity: Excessive debt can negatively impact your credit score, making it more difficult to secure loans or obtain favorable interest rates in the future.

Strategies for debt reduction:

3.To achieve financial freedom, it is essential to develop a plan for debt reduction. Here are some effective strategies:

• Prioritize debt repayment: Identify your outstanding debts and prioritize them based on interest rates and balances. Consider using the avalanche or snowball method to tackle debt. The avalanche method involves paying off high-interest debts first, while the snowball method focuses on paying off the smallest debts first for psychological motivation.

• Create a debt repayment plan: Develop a realistic debt repayment plan that fits your financial situation. Determine how much you can allocate towards debt repayment each month and stick to the plan consistently. Consider negotiating lower interest rates or exploring debt consolidation options to make the process more manageable.

• Reduce unnecessary expenses: Analyze your budget and identify areas where you can cut back on expenses. Channel the money saved towards debt repayment. Small adjustments, such as reducing dining out or entertainment expenses, can make a significant difference in your debt reduction journey.

● Increase income: Explore opportunities to increase your income. This could involve negotiating a raise, taking on a side hustle, or monetizing a hobby. The additional income can be used to accelerate debt repayment.

● Seek professional advice: If you're struggling with significant debt, consider seeking professional advice from credit counseling agencies or financial advisors. They can provide guidance on debt management strategies, negotiate with creditors on your behalf, and help you develop a personalized plan for debt reduction.

Wealth building strategies:

4.Once you have a plan for debt reduction in place, it's crucial to focus on building wealth. Here are some strategies to consider:

● Save and invest: Allocate a portion of your income towards savings and investments. Set aside money for emergencies, retirement, and other financial goals. Make informed investment decisions based on your risk tolerance and financial objectives.

● Diversify your investments: Spread your investments across different asset classes to minimize risk. Consider investing in stocks, bonds, real estate, and other investment vehicles. Diversification can help protect your wealth and potentially generate higher returns.

• Continuously educate yourself: Stay informed about personal finance and investment strategies. Read books, follow financial news, and attend seminars or workshops to expand your knowledge. The more you learn, the better equipped you'll be to make wise financial decisions.

• Seek professional advice: Consider consulting with a financial advisor who can provide personalized guidance tailored to your financial situation and goals. They can help you develop a comprehensive wealth-building plan and adjust it as needed based on market conditions and your changing circumstances.

• Set financial goals: Define specific financial goals that you want to achieve. Whether it's saving for a down payment on a house, starting a business, or retiring comfortably, having clear goals provides direction and motivation. Break down your goals into smaller milestones and track your progress regularly.

• Live below your means: Adopt a frugal mindset and live below your means. Avoid unnecessary expenses and prioritize saving and investing over excessive spending. By spending less than you earn, you create a surplus that can be allocated towards wealth building.

• Leverage the power of compound interest: Start investing early to take advantage of the power of compound interest. Even small, regular contributions to investment accounts can grow significantly over time. Let your investments compound and work for you.

- Take calculated risks: Building wealth often involves taking calculated risks. Educate yourself about investment opportunities and assess the potential risks and rewards. Be willing to step out of your comfort zone and make informed decisions based on your financial goals.

- Review and adjust your plan: Regularly review your financial plan and adjust it as necessary. Financial circumstances, market conditions, and personal goals can change over time. Stay proactive and make necessary adjustments to keep your wealth-building journey on track.

Conclusion:

Chapter 28 emphasizes the importance of debt reduction and wealth building in achieving long-term financial stability and prosperity. By effectively managing and reducing debt, you can free up resources to invest in wealth-building strategies. Prioritize debt repayment, reduce unnecessary expenses, and seek professional advice if needed. Once you've tackled your debt, focus on building wealth through saving, investing, and smart financial decisions. Set clear goals, diversify your investments, and continuously educate yourself. Remember, building wealth takes time, patience, and discipline. Stay committed to your financial plan, make informed decisions, and enjoy the journey towards financial freedom and abundance.

Chapter 29: Investments and passive income streams.

———

Introduction:

In Chapter 29, we delve into the world of investments and passive income streams. Investing wisely and generating passive income are key strategies for building wealth and achieving financial independence. This chapter will explore various investment options and passive income sources, helping you make informed decisions to grow your wealth.

Understanding investments:

1.Investing involves allocating money to different assets with the expectation of earning a return over time. Here are some common investment options:

● Stocks: Investing in individual stocks allows you to become a partial owner of a company and benefit from its success.

● Bonds: Bonds are fixed-income securities where you lend money to governments or corporations in exchange for regular interest payments.

● Mutual funds: Mutual funds pool money from multiple investors to invest in a diversified portfolio of stocks, bonds, or other assets.

- Real estate: Real estate investment involves purchasing properties with the goal of generating rental income or appreciation.

- Exchange-traded funds (ETFs): ETFs are similar to mutual funds but trade on stock exchanges like individual stocks.

Building an investment portfolio:

2.To build a successful investment portfolio, consider the following steps:

- Define your goals: Determine your investment goals, whether it's long-term growth, income generation, or a combination of both.

- Assess your risk tolerance: Understand your risk tolerance to determine the appropriate asset allocation for your portfolio. Generally, higher-risk investments offer higher potential returns but also greater volatility.

- Diversify your investments: Spread your investments across different asset classes and sectors to minimize risk. Diversification helps protect your portfolio from the impact of a single investment's performance.

- Regularly monitor and rebalance: Keep a close eye on your investments and make adjustments as needed. Rebalance your portfolio periodically to maintain the desired asset allocation.

Passive income streams:

3.Passive income refers to money earned with little or no effort on your part. Here are some passive income streams to consider:

- Rental properties: Owning and renting out properties can provide a steady stream of rental income.

- Dividend stocks: Invest in stocks that pay regular dividends, allowing you to earn income from your investments.

- Peer-to-peer lending: Participate in peer-to-peer lending platforms where you can lend money to individuals or small businesses and earn interest.

- Royalties: If you have creative works like books, music, or artwork, you can earn royalties from their use or sale.

- Affiliate marketing: Promote products or services and earn a commission for each sale or referral made through your unique affiliate link.

Risks and considerations:

4.While investments and passive income streams offer great potential, it's important to be aware of the risks involved:

- Market volatility: Investments can fluctuate in value due to market conditions, economic factors, or company-specific events.

- Research and due diligence: Before investing, conduct thorough research and due diligence to understand the potential risks and rewards.

- Time and effort: While passive income streams require less active involvement than traditional employment, they may still require initial effort and ongoing management.

- Diversification: Diversify your passive income streams to reduce reliance on a single source and protect against potential income fluctuations.

Conclusion:

Chapter 29 highlights the importance of investments and passive income streams in building wealth and achieving financial freedom. By understanding different investment options, building a diversified portfolio, and exploring passive income sources, you can create multiple streams of income and grow your wealth over time. Remember to assess your risk tolerance, conduct thorough research, and regularly monitor your investments and passive income streams. By making informed decisions and staying proactive, you can leverage the power of investments and passive income to secure your financial future.

Chapter 30: Money mindset and financial goals.

―――――

I ntroduction:

In Chapter 30, we explore the importance of cultivating a healthy money mindset and setting clear financial goals. Your mindset and attitudes towards money play a significant role in your financial success. By developing a positive money mindset and setting realistic financial goals, you can take control of your finances and work towards achieving financial abundance.

Understanding your money mindset:

1.Your money mindset refers to your beliefs, attitudes, and emotions surrounding money. It influences your financial decisions, behaviors, and relationship with money. Here are some key aspects to consider:

● Abundance vs. scarcity mindset: An abundance mindset believes that there is enough wealth and opportunities for everyone, while a scarcity mindset focuses on limitations and fears of lack. Cultivating an abundance mindset helps you see possibilities and open yourself up to financial abundance.

● Identifying limiting beliefs: Uncover any limiting beliefs you may have about money, such as "money is evil" or "I'll never be rich." Challenge these beliefs and replace them with empowering thoughts that support your financial growth.

• Money and self-worth: Recognize that your self-worth is not determined by your financial situation. Separate your sense of self-worth from your bank account balance and focus on your inherent value as a person.

• Gratitude and financial well-being: Practice gratitude for the money you have and the opportunities it provides. Gratitude shifts your focus to abundance and attracts more positive financial experiences into your life.

Setting financial goals:

2.Setting clear financial goals provides direction and motivation for your financial journey. Here's how to set effective financial goals:

• Identify your priorities: Reflect on your values and what matters most to you. Determine your short-term and long-term financial priorities, such as saving for a down payment, paying off debt, or retiring comfortably.

• Make SMART goals: Ensure your goals are Specific, Measurable, Achievable, Relevant, and Time-bound (SMART). For example, instead of a vague goal like "save money," set a SMART goal like "save $10,000 for a vacation within one year."

• Break it down: Break down your larger financial goals into smaller, actionable steps. This makes them more attainable and allows you to track your progress along the way.

• Review and adjust: Regularly review your financial goals and make adjustments as needed. Life circumstances and priorities may change, so remain flexible and update your goals accordingly.

Developing financial habits:

3.To align your mindset with your financial goals, it's crucial to develop positive financial habits. Here are some habits to cultivate:

● Budgeting: Create a budget that aligns with your financial goals. Track your income, expenses, and savings to ensure you're on the right track.

● Saving and investing: Cultivate a habit of saving a portion of your income regularly. Consider automating savings and investment contributions to make it easier.

● Spending mindfully: Practice mindful spending by evaluating your purchases and distinguishing between wants and needs. Make intentional decisions that align with your financial goals.

● Continuous learning: Stay informed about personal finance, investing, and money management. Read books, follow financial blogs, and seek out educational resources to expand your financial knowledge.

● Surround yourself with positive influences: Surround yourself with individuals who have a positive money mindset and share similar financial goals. Their support and encouragement can reinforce your own financial growth.

Conclusion:

Chapter 30 emphasizes the significance of developing a healthy money mindset and setting clear financial goals. By cultivating an abundance mindset, identifying and challenging limiting beliefs, and practicing gratitude, you can create a positive relationship with money. Additionally, setting SMART financial goals and developing positive financial habits will help you make progress towards achieving financial success. Remember that your money mindset is a lifelong journey,

continually nurture and develop it. Stay committed to your financial goals, regularly review and adjust them, and celebrate your achievements along the way.

As you continue on your financial journey, remember that money is a tool that can empower you to live a fulfilling and abundant life. Cultivate a mindset of abundance, gratitude, and self-worth, knowing that you have the ability to create financial freedom and security. Stay focused on your financial goals, make informed decisions, and seek support and guidance when needed.

By embracing a positive money mindset and setting clear financial goals, you can take control of your financial future and create a life of financial abundance and fulfillment. Your mindset and goals will guide your financial decisions and behaviors, leading you towards greater financial success and well-being. Start today by examining your beliefs, setting meaningful financial goals, and taking proactive steps towards achieving them.

Remember, your money mindset is within your control. Choose to believe in your ability to create wealth, adopt empowering beliefs, and take consistent action towards your financial goals. With a positive money mindset and clear financial goals, you can transform your relationship with money and create a life of financial freedom and abundance. Embrace the journey and enjoy the rewards that come with aligning your mindset and goals with your financial aspirations.

Chapter 31: The importance of lifelong learning.

——

I ntroduction:

In Chapter 31, we explore the significance of lifelong learning and its impact on personal growth, professional development, and overall well-being. Lifelong learning refers to the continuous pursuit of knowledge, skills, and personal development throughout one's life. In an ever-changing world, adopting a mindset of lifelong learning is crucial for staying relevant, adaptable, and fulfilling your potential.

Adapting to a changing world:

1.We live in a dynamic world where new technologies, industries, and knowledge emerge at a rapid pace. Lifelong learning allows us to adapt to these changes and embrace new opportunities. By continually acquiring knowledge and skills, we can navigate the complexities of modern life and remain competitive in the workforce.

Personal growth and development:

2.Lifelong learning fosters personal growth and development by expanding our horizons, challenging our beliefs, and broadening our perspectives. It encourages self-reflection, critical thinking, and a thirst for knowledge. Through learning, we discover new interests, explore different cultures, and gain a deeper understanding of ourselves and the world around us.

Professional advancement:

3.In today's professional landscape, continuous learning is essential for career advancement. Acquiring new skills, staying updated with industry trends, and expanding your knowledge base can enhance your professional capabilities and open doors to new opportunities. Lifelong learners are often sought after by employers for their adaptability, curiosity, and ability to embrace change.

Cognitive benefits:

4.Engaging in lifelong learning has numerous cognitive benefits. Research has shown that learning new things stimulates brain activity, improves memory, and enhances cognitive function. It helps keep the mind sharp, reducing the risk of cognitive decline and age-related disorders. Lifelong learning is like a mental workout that keeps our brains healthy and active.

Personal fulfillment and well-being:

5.Lifelong learning brings a sense of personal fulfillment and satisfaction. It allows us to pursue our passions, explore our creativity, and discover new talents. Learning new skills or subjects can ignite a sense of achievement and boost self-confidence. Moreover, the process of learning keeps us engaged, curious, and connected, leading to improved mental and emotional well-being.

Embracing continuous improvement:

6.Lifelong learning instills a mindset of continuous improvement. It encourages us to seek feedback, learn from mistakes, and embrace challenges. By adopting a growth mindset, we believe in our ability to develop and evolve throughout our lives. Lifelong learners are not afraid to step outside their comfort zones and embrace new learning opportunities.

Learning in various formats:

7.Lifelong learning takes many forms, including formal education, online courses, workshops, reading books, attending seminars, and engaging in practical experiences. The availability of online learning platforms and resources has made lifelong learning more accessible and convenient than ever before. Embrace various learning formats that suit your preferences and lifestyle.

Cultivating curiosity and wonder:

8.Lifelong learning nurtures curiosity and a sense of wonder. It encourages us to ask questions, seek answers, and explore the unknown. By approaching the world with curiosity, we develop a lifelong love for learning and an insatiable appetite for knowledge. Cultivating curiosity leads to a richer, more meaningful life.

Conclusion:

Chapter 31 highlights the importance of lifelong learning as a key driver of personal growth, professional development, and overall well-being. By embracing a mindset of continuous learning, we can adapt to a changing world, unlock our full potential, and lead fulfilling lives. Whether it's acquiring new skills, expanding our knowledge, or exploring our passions, lifelong learning empowers us to thrive in a dynamic and ever-evolving world. Embrace the journey of lifelong learning and unlock the limitless possibilities it offers.

Chapter 32: Developing self-discipline.

———

Introduction:

In Chapter 32, we delve into the importance of self-discipline and its role in personal growth, goal achievement, and overall success. Self-discipline is the ability to control and direct our actions, thoughts, and emotions towards achieving desired outcomes. It is a fundamental trait that enables us to overcome obstacles, make consistent progress, and lead a disciplined and purposeful life.

Understanding self-discipline:

1.Self-discipline is the foundation of self-control and willpower. It involves making conscious choices, delaying gratification, and staying focused on long-term goals rather than succumbing to short-term impulses. It requires commitment, perseverance, and the ability to prioritize and make sacrifices for the greater good.

Goal achievement and success:

2.Self-discipline is instrumental in achieving goals and attaining success. It provides the necessary structure and framework to stay on track, make consistent progress, and overcome challenges. With self-discipline, you can break down larger goals into smaller, manageable tasks, establish routines and habits that support your goals, and maintain the motivation and consistency required for long-term success.

Building habits and rituals:

3.Self-discipline is closely tied to building habits and rituals. By consistently engaging in positive habits, you create a structure that supports your goals and eliminates the need for constant decision-making. Habits such as regular exercise, healthy eating, and productive work routines become automatic, freeing up mental energy and strengthening your self-discipline.

Delaying gratification:

4.One of the key components of self-discipline is the ability to delay gratification. It means resisting immediate temptations and staying focused on long-term rewards. By practicing delayed gratification, you can make choices that align with your goals, whether it's saving money instead of splurging, studying instead of procrastinating, or putting in extra effort to achieve higher quality results.

Overcoming procrastination:

5.Procrastination is the arch-nemesis of self-discipline. It hinders progress, creates unnecessary stress, and sabotages goal attainment. Developing self-discipline helps overcome procrastination by cultivating a sense of responsibility, breaking tasks into smaller, manageable chunks, and setting deadlines and accountability measures. By taking consistent action and staying committed, you can overcome the allure of procrastination and make progress towards your goals.

Managing distractions:

6.In today's digitally connected world, distractions abound. Self-discipline is vital for managing distractions and staying focused on important tasks. It involves setting boundaries, practicing mindfulness, and developing strategies to minimize distractions. By consciously directing your attention and avoiding time-wasting activities, you can optimize your productivity and accomplish more in less time.

Strengthening willpower:

7.Self-discipline and willpower go hand in hand. Willpower is the mental strength and determination to make choices aligned with your goals, even when faced with temptations or obstacles. Like a muscle, willpower can be strengthened through consistent practice. By gradually increasing the demands on your self-control, practicing mindfulness and self-awareness, and nurturing a positive mindset, you can cultivate a stronger willpower and enhance your self-discipline.

Accountability and support:

8.Accountability and support are crucial for developing self-discipline. Surround yourself with individuals who share your values and goals, and who can provide encouragement and support along your journey. Find an accountability partner or join a group that holds you responsible for your actions. Having external accountability helps reinforce self-discipline and keeps you motivated and on track.

Conclusion:

Chapter 32 highlights the significance of self-discipline in personal growth, goal achievement, and overall success. By cultivating self-discipline, you can harness your willpower, overcome obstacles, and make consistent progress towards your goals. Self-discipline empowers you to

take control of your actions and choices, allowing you to align them with your long-term aspirations. It provides the necessary structure and focus to stay on track, even when faced with distractions or obstacles.

Developing self-discipline requires practice and commitment. Here are some strategies to strengthen your self-discipline:

1.Set clear goals: Clearly define your goals and break them down into actionable steps. Having a clear direction and purpose will help you stay motivated and focused.

2.Create a routine: Establish a daily routine that includes specific time blocks for tasks related to your goals. By incorporating regular and consistent actions into your routine, you build discipline and make progress towards your objectives.

3.Prioritize and eliminate distractions: Identify the activities or habits that distract you from your goals and find ways to minimize or eliminate them. Create an environment that supports your focus and minimizes temptations.

4.Practice time management: Learn to manage your time effectively by setting deadlines, prioritizing tasks, and avoiding procrastination. Break larger tasks into smaller, manageable chunks and allocate dedicated time for each.

5.Develop healthy habits: Cultivate healthy habits that support your overall well-being and contribute to your personal growth. This includes activities like regular exercise, proper nutrition, adequate sleep, and mindfulness practices.

6.Practice self-control: Train yourself to resist immediate gratification and make choices that align with your long-term goals. This could involve delaying small rewards in favor of more significant achievements.

7.Learn from setbacks: Embrace setbacks as learning opportunities and use them to strengthen your resolve. Analyze the factors that led to the setback and find ways to prevent or overcome them in the future.

8.Seek accountability: Find an accountability partner or join a supportive community where you can share your goals and progress. Being held accountable by others can increase your commitment and motivation.

9.Practice mindfulness: Cultivate mindfulness to enhance self-awareness and self-control. Be present in the moment and observe your thoughts, emotions, and behaviors without judgment. This can help you make conscious choices aligned with your goals.

10.Celebrate small wins: Acknowledge and celebrate your achievements along the way. Recognizing your progress, no matter how small, boosts motivation and reinforces your commitment to self-discipline.

Remember, developing self-discipline is a journey that requires patience and perseverance. Start by making small changes and gradually build upon them. With consistent effort and a positive mindset, you can strengthen your self-discipline and unlock your true potential.

Conclusion:

Chapter 32 emphasizes the importance of developing self-discipline in order to achieve personal and professional success. By cultivating self-discipline, setting clear goals, establishing routines, managing time effectively, and practicing self-control, you can overcome challenges, stay focused, and make consistent progress towards your aspirations. Self-discipline is a valuable trait that empowers you to take charge of your life and accomplish your goals with determination and resilience. Embrace the principles of self-discipline and experience the transformation it brings to your life.

Chapter 33: Overcoming procrastination.

———

Introduction:

In Chapter 33, we explore the topic of procrastination, its detrimental effects on personal and professional growth, and strategies to overcome it. Procrastination is the act of delaying or postponing tasks or actions that need to be accomplished. It often stems from a combination of factors such as fear, lack of motivation, overwhelm, and a tendency to prioritize short-term gratification over long-term goals. Overcoming procrastination is essential for productivity, goal attainment, and overall success.

Understanding procrastination:

1.Procrastination is more than just laziness or a lack of time management skills. It is a complex psychological behavior rooted in various underlying causes. By understanding the reasons behind your procrastination, you can address them effectively and develop strategies to overcome it.

Identifying procrastination patterns:

2.Start by identifying your personal patterns of procrastination. Notice the tasks or activities you tend to put off, the excuses you make, and the emotions that arise when you consider doing those tasks. By becoming aware of these patterns, you can interrupt the cycle and take proactive steps to overcome them.

Breaking tasks into smaller steps:

3.One of the main reasons for procrastination is feeling overwhelmed by the size or complexity of a task. Break down your tasks into smaller, manageable steps. This makes them less daunting and easier to tackle. Focus on one step at a time, and celebrate your progress along the way.

Setting clear and realistic goals:

4.Procrastination often thrives in the absence of clear and realistic goals. Set specific, achievable goals for yourself, and establish deadlines to create a sense of urgency. Clear goals provide direction and motivation, making it easier to overcome the tendency to procrastinate.

Finding your motivation:

5.Discover what truly motivates you to complete a task. Identify the benefits, rewards, or consequences associated with accomplishing or not accomplishing it. Connect emotionally with the desired outcome to increase your motivation and reduce the inclination to procrastinate.

Managing time effectively:

6.Procrastination and poor time management go hand in hand. Implement effective time management techniques such as prioritizing tasks, creating schedules, and utilizing productivity tools. By managing your time wisely, you can minimize the opportunity for procrastination to creep in.

Overcoming perfectionism:

7.Perfectionism often fuels procrastination as individuals fear not being able to meet their own high standards. Understand that perfection is unattainable, and focus on progress rather than perfection. Embrace the concept of "done is better than perfect" to overcome the tendency to delay tasks unnecessarily.

Utilizing time-blocking and pomodoro technique:

8.Time-blocking involves allocating dedicated blocks of time for specific tasks or activities. The Pomodoro Technique is a time-management method that breaks work into intervals, typically 25 minutes, followed by short breaks. These techniques help create structure and enhance focus, making it easier to avoid procrastination.

Eliminating distractions:

9.Identify and minimize distractions that contribute to procrastination. Create a conducive environment for work by reducing or eliminating distractions such as social media, excessive noise, or clutter. Consider using website blockers or implementing specific rules to keep distractions at bay.

Cultivating discipline and self-accountability:

10.Develop discipline and hold yourself accountable for your actions. Establish routines, create to-do lists, and stick to deadlines. Engage in self-reflection to understand the consequences of procrastination and the benefits of taking timely action.

Conclusion:

Chapter 33 emphasizes the detrimental impact of procrastination on personal and professional growth and provides strategies to overcome it. By understanding the root causes of procrastination, breaking tasks into smaller steps, setting clear goals, finding motivation, managing time effectively, overcoming perfectionism, and utilizing techniques like time-blocking and the Pomodoro Technique, you can effectively combat procrastination. Additionally, eliminating distractions, cultivating discipline, and holding yourself accountable for your actions are essential in overcoming this common obstacle.

Overcoming procrastination requires self-awareness, determination, and a willingness to change your mindset and habits. It's important to remember that procrastination is a habit that can be unlearned. By implementing the strategies outlined in this chapter consistently, you can develop a proactive approach to task completion and achieve greater productivity and success.

It's also worth noting that overcoming procrastination is a journey, and setbacks may occur along the way. However, by learning from those setbacks and staying committed to your goals, you can build resilience and continue making progress. Celebrate your achievements, no matter how small, and use them as fuel to keep moving forward.

In conclusion, Chapter 33 provides valuable insights into understanding procrastination and offers practical strategies to overcome it. By applying these techniques and adopting a proactive mindset, you can break free from the grips of procrastination and unlock your full potential. Remember, the time to take action is now, and by conquering procrastination, you can create a path towards personal and professional fulfillment.

Chapter 34: Integrating new habits.

———

I ntroduction:

Chapter 34 delves into the process of integrating new habits into your daily life. Habits play a significant role in shaping our behaviors and ultimately determining our level of success. Whether it's adopting healthier lifestyle choices, enhancing productivity, or improving relationships, the ability to form and sustain new habits is crucial. This chapter explores effective strategies for integrating new habits and creating lasting positive change.

Start small:

> 1.When introducing a new habit, it's essential to start small. Begin with a habit that is easily achievable and requires minimal effort. This approach helps build momentum and confidence, setting the foundation for more substantial changes later on.

Define your why:

> 2.Understanding the underlying motivation behind the habit you want to cultivate is key to its integration. Clearly define why the habit is important to you and how it aligns with your values and long-term goals. This sense of purpose will provide the necessary drive and commitment to stay consistent.

Create a cue:

3.Cues serve as triggers that prompt you to engage in the desired habit. Identify a specific cue that is associated with the habit you want to adopt. It could be a specific time of day, a visual reminder, or linking the habit to an existing routine. The cue helps establish a mental connection and signals your brain to initiate the behavior.

Build a routine:

4.Incorporate the new habit into a daily or weekly routine. Consistency is key when integrating a new behavior into your life. Designate a specific time or day for practicing the habit and make it a non-negotiable part of your schedule. Over time, the habit becomes automatic and requires less conscious effort.

Track your progress:

5.Keeping track of your progress is essential for maintaining motivation and accountability. Use a habit tracker or journal to record your daily or weekly adherence to the habit. This visual representation of your progress will reinforce the habit and provide a sense of accomplishment.

Use implementation intentions:

6.Implementation intentions are specific if-then statements that mentally prepare you for potential obstacles. Anticipate challenges that may arise and create a plan for how you will overcome them. By having a predetermined response to obstacles, you increase your chances of staying on track with the new habit.

Seek support and accountability:

7.Enlist the support of family, friends, or a mentor who can provide encouragement and hold you accountable. Share your habit-building journey with them and ask for their support in keeping you motivated and on track. Consider joining a community or finding an accountability partner who shares similar goals.

Practice mindfulness:

8.Mindfulness can enhance your ability to integrate new habits by bringing awareness to your thoughts, emotions, and behaviors. Be fully present in the moment as you engage in the habit, focusing on the sensations and benefits it brings. Mindfulness helps reinforce the habit and strengthens your commitment to it.

Celebrate milestones:

9.Celebrate your achievements and milestones along the way. Recognize and reward yourself for successfully integrating the habit into your life. Celebrations provide positive reinforcement and reinforce the habit as a source of joy and satisfaction.

Persevere and be patient:

10.Integrating new habits takes time and effort. Be patient with yourself and understand that setbacks are a normal part of the process. If you slip up, acknowledge it, learn from it, and recommit to the habit. Perseverance and consistency will ultimately lead to successful habit integration.

Conclusion:

Chapter 34 highlights the importance of integrating new habits and provides practical strategies for successful habit formation. By starting small, defining your why, creating cues and routines, tracking progress, using implementation intentions, seeking support, practicing mindfulness, and celebrating milestones, you can effectively integrate new habits into your life.

Remember, habit integration is a gradual process that requires patience, persistence, and self-reflection. It's important to approach habit integration with a growth mindset and embrace the journey of personal development.

Throughout the process, it's crucial to stay focused on your long-term goals and maintain a positive attitude. Recognize that setbacks and challenges are inevitable, but they shouldn't discourage you from continuing your efforts. Instead, view them as opportunities to learn and adjust your approach.

As you integrate new habits, be mindful of your progress and make adjustments as needed. Reflect on what is working well and what can be improved. This self-awareness will help you refine your strategies and make the necessary adjustments to ensure long-term success.

Additionally, staying consistent and committed to your habits is key. Consistency creates a sense of reliability and reinforces the habit in your daily life. Even on days when motivation is low, remind yourself of the benefits and the positive impact that the habit will have on your life.

It's also important to be flexible and adaptable in your approach. Life is dynamic, and circumstances may change. Adaptability allows you to modify your habits to fit different situations while still staying true to your overall goals and values.

Finally, be kind to yourself throughout the process. Habits take time to form, and it's natural to experience ups and downs along the way. Practice self-compassion and understand that each step forward, no matter how small, is a step in the right direction.

In conclusion, Chapter 34 emphasizes the significance of integrating new habits into your life for personal growth and transformation. By following the strategies outlined in this chapter and maintaining a positive mindset, you can successfully incorporate new habits that align with your goals and values. Remember, the journey of habit integration is unique to each individual, so embrace the process, stay committed, and celebrate your progress along the way.

Chapter 35: Long-term personal growth.

─────

Introduction:

Chapter 35 explores the concept of long-term personal growth and provides insights into sustaining continuous development over time. While personal growth is a lifelong journey, it's essential to have strategies and frameworks in place to ensure ongoing progress and transformation. This chapter offers guidance on how to cultivate long-term personal growth and create a fulfilling and purposeful life.

Embrace lifelong learning:

1.One of the key pillars of long-term personal growth is embracing lifelong learning. Continuously seek knowledge and expand your skills in various areas of interest. Engage in formal education, attend workshops and seminars, read books, and explore new subjects. Embracing a curious and open mindset allows for ongoing personal and intellectual development.

Set meaningful goals:

2.Long-term personal growth requires setting meaningful and purpose-driven goals. Take the time to reflect on what truly matters to you and align your goals with your values and aspirations. Set both short-term and long-term goals that challenge you and inspire growth. Regularly review and adjust your goals as you progress on your personal growth journey.

Cultivate resilience:

3.Resilience is a vital attribute for long-term personal growth. Develop the ability to bounce back from setbacks and challenges. Embrace failures as learning opportunities and use them to fuel your growth. Build a strong support system of family, friends, or mentors who can provide guidance and encouragement during tough times.

Practice self-reflection:

4.Regular self-reflection allows you to gain insights into your experiences and make conscious choices for personal growth. Set aside dedicated time for introspection, journaling, or meditation. Reflect on your actions, values, and beliefs. Identify areas for improvement and develop strategies to overcome obstacles.

Foster meaningful relationships:

5.Healthy and supportive relationships contribute to long-term personal growth. Surround yourself with individuals who inspire and challenge you. Seek mentors or coaches who can provide guidance and accountability. Engage in meaningful conversations and collaborative endeavors that foster personal and professional development.

Embrace change and adaptability:

6.Personal growth requires embracing change and being adaptable to new circumstances. Life is dynamic, and opportunities for growth often come in unexpected forms. Embrace uncertainty, step out of your comfort zone, and embrace new experiences. Adaptability allows you to navigate challenges and seize opportunities for growth.

Practice self-care:

7.Taking care of your physical, mental, and emotional well-being is crucial for long-term personal growth. Prioritize self-care activities such as exercise, proper nutrition, restful sleep, and stress management techniques. Engage in activities that bring you joy and recharge your energy. Self-care provides the foundation for personal growth and helps maintain balance in your life.

Seek feedback and continuous improvement:

8.Regularly seek feedback from trusted sources to gain insights into areas where you can improve. Actively seek constructive criticism and use it as a tool for growth. Embrace a growth mindset that values continuous improvement and see challenges as opportunities to learn and grow.

Give back and contribute:

9.Long-term personal growth is not just about individual development; it also involves giving back to others and contributing to society. Find ways to make a positive impact through volunteering, mentoring, or supporting causes you believe in. Sharing your knowledge and experiences not only benefits others but also deepens your own growth.

Celebrate milestones and progress:

10.Acknowledge and celebrate your achievements and milestones along the way. Take time to reflect on how far you've come and appreciate the progress you've made.

Celebrating your growth reinforces a positive mindset and motivates you to continue on your personal growth journey.

Conclusion:

Chapter 35 emphasizes the importance of long-term personal growth and provides strategies for sustaining continuous development. By embracing lifelong learning, setting meaningful goals, cultivating resilience, practicing self-reflection, fostering meaningful relationships, embracing change and adaptability, practicing self-care, seeking feedback, and giving back, you can create a solid foundation for long-term personal growth.

Remember, personal growth is not a destination but a continuous journey. It requires commitment, perseverance, and an unwavering belief in your ability to evolve and improve. Embrace the challenges and opportunities that come your way, and never stop seeking ways to expand your knowledge, skills, and perspectives.

As you embark on your long-term personal growth journey, keep the following principles in mind:

1.Patience and persistence: Personal growth takes time, and it's important to be patient with yourself. Recognize that progress may be gradual, and setbacks are natural. Stay persistent and committed to your growth despite obstacles or temporary setbacks.

2.Embrace curiosity: Cultivate a sense of curiosity and a thirst for knowledge. Be open to new ideas, perspectives, and experiences. Continually seek opportunities to learn and grow, both within and outside your comfort zone.

3.Reflect and learn: Regular self-reflection is crucial for long-term personal growth. Set aside dedicated time to evaluate your progress, identify areas for improvement, and make necessary adjustments. Learn from your experiences and apply those lessons to future endeavors.

4.Surround yourself with support: Build a support system of like-minded individuals who encourage and inspire you. Seek out mentors, coaches, or accountability partners who can provide guidance and support on your journey. Surrounding yourself with positive influences will fuel your motivation and help you stay on track.

5.Embrace challenges: Growth often occurs when we step outside our comfort zones and face challenges. Embrace these opportunities for growth and see them as valuable learning experiences. Develop resilience and see failures as stepping stones to success.

6.Practice self-compassion: Be kind and compassionate towards yourself throughout your personal growth journey. Acknowledge your achievements, no matter how small, and celebrate your progress. Treat yourself with the same kindness and understanding you would extend to a friend.

7.Stay flexible and adapt: Life is unpredictable, and circumstances may change. Stay flexible and adaptable in your approach to personal growth. Be willing to adjust your goals, strategies, and habits as needed. Embrace change as an opportunity for growth and embrace new possibilities.

8.Keep the momentum going: Personal growth requires consistent effort and commitment. Even when you achieve a milestone or reach a goal, don't stop there. Use that momentum to set new challenges and continue pushing yourself to new heights.

In conclusion, Chapter 35 emphasizes the significance of long-term personal growth and provides guidance on sustaining continuous development. By embracing the principles of patience, curiosity, reflection, support, embracing challenges, self-compassion, adaptability, and maintaining momentum, you can create a lifelong journey of personal growth and fulfillment. Remember, personal growth is a lifelong pursuit, and every step you take brings you closer to becoming the best version of yourself.

Chapter 36: Embracing failure and defeat.

———

I ntroduction:

Chapter 36 delves into the often uncomfortable but essential topic of embracing failure and defeat on the path of personal growth. While failure and defeat can be disheartening, they also present valuable opportunities for learning, growth, and resilience. This chapter explores the mindset and strategies needed to navigate failure and defeat in a constructive and empowering way.

Changing your perspective:

1. Failure and defeat are often viewed as negative experiences, but they can be reframed as stepping stones to success. Embrace a growth mindset that sees failure as a natural part of the learning process. Shift your perspective from seeing failure as an endpoint to viewing it as a valuable feedback mechanism that guides you towards improvement.

Learning from failure:

2. Every failure carries valuable lessons if you are willing to learn from them. Take the time to reflect on what went wrong, identify areas for improvement, and develop strategies to overcome similar challenges in the future. Use failure as an opportunity to gain insights, acquire new skills, and grow as an individual.

Building resilience:

3.Failure and defeat can test your resilience and determination. Embrace these experiences as opportunities to develop and strengthen your resilience muscles. Learn to bounce back from setbacks, adapt to changing circumstances, and persevere in the face of adversity. Building resilience equips you with the tools to face future challenges with confidence.

Embracing risk-taking:

4.Fear of failure often holds us back from taking risks and pursuing our dreams. Embrace failure as an inherent part of taking risks and stepping outside your comfort zone. Recognize that failure is not a reflection of your worth or abilities but a natural consequence of pushing boundaries and exploring new possibilities.

Cultivating self-compassion:

5.When faced with failure and defeat, it's important to practice self-compassion. Treat yourself with kindness, understanding, and forgiveness. Acknowledge that everyone experiences setbacks and that failure does not define your identity. Use self-compassion as a source of strength and motivation to keep moving forward.

Seeking support:

6.During times of failure and defeat, it's crucial to seek support from others. Surround yourself with a network of supportive individuals who can provide encouragement, guidance, and perspective. Share your experiences with trusted friends, mentors, or coaches who can offer valuable insights and help you navigate through challenging times.

Reframing failure as feedback:

7.Rather than viewing failure as a personal shortcoming, reframe it as feedback on your approach or strategy. Use failure as an opportunity to fine-tune your methods, make necessary adjustments, and grow from the experience. Shift your focus from dwelling on the failure itself to analyzing the lessons it provides.

Perseverance and persistence:

8.Failure and defeat can be discouraging, but it's important to maintain a sense of perseverance and persistence. Remember that success is often the result of multiple failures and setbacks. Stay committed to your goals, learn from each setback, and keep moving forward with determination and resilience.

Celebrating small wins:

9.While failure and defeat may overshadow your progress, it's important to celebrate small wins along the way. Recognize and appreciate the milestones, achievements, and lessons learned throughout your journey. Celebrating small wins provides motivation and reminds you of your growth and potential for future success.

Redefining success:

10.Instead of defining success solely based on external outcomes, redefine success as personal growth, resilience, and the lessons learned from failure. Shift your focus from the end result to the process of self-improvement and continuous learning. Embrace failure as an essential part of the success journey, and success will follow.

Conclusion:

Chapter 36 highlights the importance of embracing failure and defeat as valuable opportunities for growth and learning. By shifting your perspective, learning from failure, building resilience, embracing risk-taking, cultivating self-compassion, seeking support, reframing failure as feedback, practicing perseverance and persistence, celebrating small wins, and redefining success, you can transform failure and defeat into stepping stones toward personal growth and success.

It is essential to recognize that failure is not an indication of your worth or abilities but a natural part of the journey towards personal growth. Embracing failure allows you to learn valuable lessons, develop resilience, and refine your strategies. By changing your perspective and viewing failure as a temporary setback rather than a permanent defeat, you can bounce back stronger and more determined than ever.

Learning from failure requires self-reflection and a willingness to analyze what went wrong. Use failure as an opportunity to assess your approach, identify areas for improvement, and develop new strategies. Each failure brings you closer to success, as long as you are willing to learn from it and adapt your approach accordingly.

Building resilience is another crucial aspect of embracing failure. Resilience allows you to bounce back from setbacks, navigate challenges with confidence, and persevere in the face of adversity. By developing resilience, you can view failure as a temporary setback rather than an insurmountable obstacle.

Risk-taking is an inherent part of personal growth and success. Embracing failure means being willing to take risks, step outside your comfort zone, and pursue your dreams and goals. Understand that failure is a natural consequence of pushing boundaries and exploring new possibilities. Without taking risks, you limit your potential for growth and success.

Cultivating self-compassion is essential when facing failure and defeat. Treat yourself with kindness, understanding, and forgiveness. Avoid self-criticism and negative self-talk. Remember that failure does not define your worth or abilities. Practice self-compassion as a source of strength and motivation to keep moving forward.

Seeking support is crucial during times of failure and defeat. Surround yourself with a network of supportive individuals who can offer encouragement, guidance, and perspective. Share your experiences with trusted friends, mentors, or coaches who can provide valuable insights and help you navigate through challenging times. Remember that you don't have to face failure alone.

Reframing failure as feedback allows you to shift your perspective and view failure as valuable information that can guide your future actions. Rather than dwelling on the failure itself, focus on analyzing the lessons it provides. Use failure as an opportunity to fine-tune your methods, make necessary adjustments, and grow from the experience.

Perseverance and persistence are key traits when embracing failure. Understand that success is often the result of multiple failures and setbacks. Stay committed to your goals, learn from each setback, and keep moving forward with determination and resilience. Each failure brings you one step closer to achieving your desired outcome.

Celebrating small wins along the way is important to maintain motivation and recognize your progress. Even in the face of failure, there are often small achievements and milestones worth acknowledging. Celebrate these victories as they signify growth and progress on your personal journey.

Finally, redefine success as personal growth, resilience, and the lessons learned from failure. Instead of solely focusing on external outcomes, shift your perspective to appreciate the process of self-improvement and continuous learning. By redefining success, failure becomes a natural and necessary part of the journey.

In conclusion, Chapter 36 emphasizes the importance of embracing failure and defeat as opportunities for growth, learning, and resilience. By changing your perspective, learning from failure, building resilience, embracing risk-taking, cultivating self-compassion, seeking support, reframing failure as feedback, practicing perseverance and persistence, celebrating small wins, and redefining success, you can transform failure into a catalyst for personal growth and success. Embrace failure as a valuable teacher on your journey toward reaching your full potential.

Chapter 37: The art of resilient thinking and action.

─────

I ntroduction:

Chapter 37 explores the art of resilient thinking and action, focusing on developing the mindset and strategies needed to bounce back from challenges, setbacks, and adversity. Resilience is a vital skill that allows individuals to adapt, thrive, and maintain a positive outlook in the face of difficulties. This chapter will delve into the various aspects of resilient thinking and action and provide practical techniques to cultivate resilience in everyday life.

Understanding resilient thinking:

1. Resilient thinking involves developing a mindset that sees challenges as opportunities for growth and learning. It is about reframing setbacks and adversity as temporary obstacles rather than insurmountable barriers. Resilient thinkers believe in their ability to overcome difficulties and approach problems with a solution-oriented mindset.

Building emotional resilience:

2. Emotional resilience is the ability to bounce back from emotional challenges, such as stress, disappointment, or failure. It involves developing emotional awareness, managing emotions effectively, and cultivating coping strategies. By building emotional resilience, individuals can navigate through tough times with grace and maintain a positive outlook.

Cultivating optimism:

3.Optimism is a powerful mindset that fuels resilience. It involves adopting a positive outlook, focusing on possibilities, and maintaining hope even in the face of adversity. Cultivating optimism requires reframing negative thoughts, practicing gratitude, and seeking opportunities for growth in every situation.

Developing problem-solving skills:

4.Resilient individuals possess strong problem-solving skills. They approach challenges with a proactive mindset and actively seek solutions. Developing problem-solving skills involves breaking down problems into manageable steps, brainstorming creative solutions, and being open to new perspectives and ideas.

Adapting to change:

5.Resilience entails the ability to adapt to change and uncertainty. Resilient individuals embrace change as an opportunity for growth and view it as a natural part of life. They remain flexible, open-minded, and willing to adjust their plans and strategies as needed.

Cultivating self-compassion:

6.Self-compassion is an essential aspect of resilience. It involves treating oneself with kindness, understanding, and acceptance, especially during challenging times. By practicing self-compassion, individuals can cultivate a nurturing internal dialogue and bounce back from setbacks with a renewed sense of self-worth.

Building a supportive network:

7.Resilience is not built in isolation. Building a supportive network of family, friends, mentors, and colleagues provides a valuable source of emotional support, guidance, and encouragement. Surrounding oneself with positive and resilient individuals can inspire and uplift during difficult times.

Practicing mindfulness:

8.Mindfulness is a powerful tool for cultivating resilience. By practicing mindfulness, individuals develop the ability to stay present, observe their thoughts and emotions without judgment, and respond to challenges with clarity and composure. Mindfulness helps build resilience by reducing stress, enhancing emotional regulation, and promoting overall well-being.

Embracing failure as feedback:

9.Resilient thinkers view failure as an opportunity for growth and learning. They embrace failure as feedback that guides them towards improvement and adjust their strategies accordingly. Rather than being discouraged by failure, resilient individuals see it as an integral part of the journey toward success.

Taking care of physical well-being:

10.Physical well-being is closely linked to resilience. Taking care of one's physical health through regular exercise, proper nutrition, and adequate sleep provides the energy and strength needed to bounce back from challenges. Physical well-being supports mental and emotional resilience, enhancing overall resilience levels.

Conclusion:

Chapter 37 explores the art of resilient thinking and action, emphasizing the importance of cultivating a mindset that sees challenges as opportunities for growth, maintaining optimism, developing problem-solving skills, adapting to change, practicing self-compassion, building a supportive network, practicing mindfulness, embracing failure as feedback, taking care of physical well-being, and other strategies to enhance resilience. Resilient thinking and action are essential for navigating through life's ups and downs and thriving in the face of adversity.

By understanding the principles of resilient thinking, individuals can develop a mindset that enables them to bounce back from setbacks and challenges. They learn to reframe negative experiences, focusing on the lessons learned and the opportunities for growth and development. Resilient thinkers maintain a positive outlook, believing in their ability to overcome obstacles and find solutions.

Building emotional resilience is a crucial aspect of resilient thinking and action. It involves developing emotional awareness, recognizing and managing emotions effectively, and cultivating healthy coping mechanisms. By understanding their emotions and responding to them in a constructive way, individuals can navigate through difficult situations with resilience and grace.

Optimism plays a significant role in resilient thinking. It is the ability to maintain a positive outlook, even in the face of adversity. Optimistic individuals believe that setbacks are temporary and that they have the power to overcome challenges. They focus on possibilities and maintain hope, which fuels their resilience and motivates them to take action.

Developing problem-solving skills is another vital component of resilient thinking and action. Resilient individuals approach problems with a proactive mindset, seeking creative and effective solutions. They break down complex issues into smaller manageable steps, brainstorm ideas, and remain open to different perspectives. By developing problem-solving skills, individuals can navigate through challenges and find innovative solutions.

Resilient individuals are adaptable and embrace change. They understand that life is filled with uncertainties and that the ability to adapt is crucial for resilience. Adapting to change involves being flexible, open-minded, and willing to adjust plans and strategies as needed. By embracing change and seeing it as an opportunity for growth, individuals can maintain their resilience and continue moving forward.

Cultivating self-compassion is an important aspect of resilient thinking and action. Self-compassion involves treating oneself with kindness, understanding, and acceptance, especially during difficult times. Resilient individuals practice self-compassion by acknowledging their struggles, validating their emotions, and offering themselves comfort and support. By practicing self-compassion, individuals can bounce back from setbacks with renewed self-worth and resilience.

Building a supportive network is crucial for resilient thinking and action. Surrounding oneself with positive and resilient individuals provides emotional support, guidance, and encouragement during challenging times. A supportive network can offer different perspectives, share experiences, and provide a sense of belonging. By building a strong support system, individuals can enhance their resilience and feel empowered to face life's challenges.

Practicing mindfulness is an effective way to cultivate resilient thinking and action. Mindfulness involves being present in the moment, observing thoughts and emotions without judgment, and responding consciously to challenges. By practicing mindfulness, individuals develop self-awareness, emotional regulation, and the ability to respond rather than react. Mindfulness reduces stress, enhances well-being, and strengthens resilience.

Embracing failure as feedback is an integral part of resilient thinking and action. Resilient individuals view failure as an opportunity for growth and learning. They see failure as a stepping stone towards success and use it as feedback to adjust their strategies and improve. By embracing failure and reframing it as a valuable learning experience, individuals can bounce back stronger and more resilient.

Taking care of physical well-being is essential for resilience. Physical exercise, proper nutrition, and adequate sleep contribute to overall well-being and energy levels. By prioritizing physical health, individuals have the strength and vitality to face challenges and maintain resilience. Physical well-being supports mental and emotional resilience, enabling individuals to thrive in all areas of life.

In conclusion, Chapter 37 explores the art of resilient thinking and action. By cultivating a mindset that embraces challenges, maintains optimism, develops problem solving skills, adapts to change, practices self-compassion, builds a supportive network, engages in mindfulness, embraces failure as feedback, and takes care of physical well-being, individuals can enhance their resilience. Resilient thinking and action allow individuals to navigate through life's challenges, setbacks, and uncertainties with grace and determination.

Resilient individuals understand that setbacks and challenges are not permanent roadblocks but opportunities for growth and learning. They approach difficulties with a positive mindset, seeking solutions and viewing obstacles as stepping stones toward success. By reframing negative experiences, they find valuable lessons and opportunities for personal development.

Emotional resilience is a vital aspect of resilient thinking and action. It involves recognizing and managing emotions effectively, developing healthy coping mechanisms, and seeking support when needed. Resilient individuals understand their emotional triggers and respond to them in a constructive manner. They cultivate emotional intelligence and resilience, allowing them to bounce back from emotional challenges and maintain a positive outlook.

Optimism is a powerful mindset that fuels resilience. Resilient individuals believe in their ability to overcome obstacles and maintain hope even in the face of adversity. They focus on possibilities rather than limitations, finding silver linings and opportunities for growth. Optimism provides the motivation and drive to persevere and overcome challenges.

Developing problem-solving skills is crucial for resilient thinking and action. Resilient individuals approach problems with a proactive mindset, seeking creative and effective solutions. They break down complex issues into manageable steps, brainstorm ideas, and consider different perspectives. By developing strong problem-solving skills, individuals can overcome challenges and adapt to new situations with ease.

Resilient individuals embrace change and adapt to new circumstances. They understand that change is inevitable and approach it with flexibility and an open mind. They adjust their plans and strategies accordingly, seeking new opportunities and possibilities. By embracing change, they develop the resilience needed to thrive in a rapidly changing world.

Cultivating self-compassion is an essential aspect of resilient thinking and action. Resilient individuals treat themselves with kindness, understanding, and acceptance, especially during difficult times. They acknowledge their struggles, validate their emotions, and practice self-care. By practicing self-compassion, individuals can bounce back from setbacks and failures with a renewed sense of self-worth and resilience.

Building a supportive network is vital for resilient thinking and action. Surrounding oneself with positive and resilient individuals provides emotional support, guidance, and encouragement. A supportive network offers different perspectives, shares experiences, and provides a sense of belonging. By building strong relationships and seeking support from others, individuals can enhance their resilience and find strength during challenging times.

Practicing mindfulness is a powerful tool for cultivating resilient thinking and action. Mindfulness involves being fully present in the moment, observing thoughts and emotions without judgment, and responding consciously to challenges. By practicing mindfulness, individuals develop self-awareness, emotional regulation, and the ability to respond effectively to stressors. Mindfulness reduces stress, enhances well-being, and strengthens resilience.

Embracing failure as feedback is a key aspect of resilient thinking and action. Resilient individuals view failure as an opportunity for growth and learning. They see failure as a natural part of the journey toward success and use it as feedback to adjust their strategies and improve. By embracing failure and learning from it, individuals can bounce back stronger and more resilient.

Taking care of physical well-being is crucial for overall resilience. Regular exercise, proper nutrition, and adequate sleep contribute to physical health and energy levels. By prioritizing physical well-being, individuals have the strength and stamina to face challenges and maintain resilience. Physical health supports mental and emotional well-being, enabling individuals to thrive in all areas of life.

In conclusion, Chapter 37 emphasizes the importance of resilient thinking and action. By cultivating a mindset that embraces challenges, maintains optimism, develops problem-solving.

Chapter 38: Bouncing back from setbacks and disappointments.

―――

I ntroduction:

Chapter 38 delves into the topic of bouncing back from setbacks and disappointments, exploring strategies and techniques to overcome adversity and regain momentum. Life is full of unexpected twists and turns, and setbacks and disappointments are inevitable. However, how we respond to these challenges determines our ability to bounce back and continue moving forward. This chapter focuses on building resilience, embracing a growth mindset, and developing effective strategies to navigate through setbacks and disappointments.

Understanding setbacks and disappointments:

1.Setbacks and disappointments are part of life's journey. They can arise in various areas such as personal relationships, career, education, or personal goals. Understanding that setbacks and disappointments are common experiences helps to normalize and accept them as a natural part of life.

Cultivating resilience:

2.Resilience is the ability to bounce back from adversity. It involves developing a mindset that sees setbacks and disappointments as temporary and solvable challenges. Resilient individuals believe in their ability to overcome obstacles and view setbacks as opportunities for growth. By cultivating resilience, individuals can build their emotional strength and adaptability to navigate through difficult times.

Embracing a growth mindset:

3.A growth mindset is essential when facing setbacks and disappointments. It involves believing that abilities and intelligence can be developed through dedication and hard work. With a growth mindset, individuals see setbacks as learning opportunities rather than failures. They understand that setbacks are stepping stones to progress and use them to improve and grow.

Managing emotions:

4.Dealing with setbacks and disappointments can trigger a range of emotions such as frustration, anger, sadness, or self-doubt. It is crucial to acknowledge and process these emotions in a healthy way. By practicing self-awareness and emotional regulation techniques, individuals can manage their emotions effectively and prevent them from derailing their progress.

Reframing setbacks:

5.Reframing setbacks involves shifting the perspective from a negative outlook to a positive and growth-oriented one. It entails focusing on the lessons learned, the opportunities for improvement, and the potential for personal growth. By reframing setbacks, individuals can see them as valuable experiences that contribute to their resilience and success.

Seeking support:

6.During challenging times, it is essential to seek support from friends, family, mentors, or professional networks. Sharing experiences and emotions with trusted individuals can provide comfort, guidance, and fresh perspectives. Supportive individuals can offer encouragement, advice, and help in developing strategies to overcome setbacks and disappointments.

Learning from failure:

7.Failure is often a part of setbacks and disappointments. However, it is essential to view failure as a learning experience rather than a permanent defeat. By reflecting on failures, individuals can identify areas for improvement, adjust their strategies, and develop resilience. Learning from failure is a valuable tool for growth and can pave the way for future success.

Setting realistic expectations:

8.Setbacks and disappointments can occur when expectations are unrealistic or unattainable. It is crucial to set realistic goals and expectations to avoid unnecessary disappointment. By setting achievable goals, individuals can maintain motivation and avoid feeling overwhelmed by setbacks.

Taking action and planning:

9.After experiencing setbacks and disappointments, taking action is crucial to regain momentum. It involves creating a plan of action and setting achievable steps towards overcoming the challenges. By breaking down the process into manageable tasks, individuals can regain a sense of control and make progress towards their goals.

Cultivating self-compassion:

10. Self-compassion is essential when dealing with setbacks and disappointments. It involves treating oneself with kindness, understanding, and acceptance. Rather than engaging in self-blame or harsh self-criticism, individuals practice self-compassion by offering support and encouragement to themselves. They acknowledge that setbacks and disappointments are a part of life and treat themselves with the same kindness and compassion they would offer to a friend facing similar challenges. By cultivating self-compassion, individuals can bounce back from setbacks with a renewed sense of self-worth and resilience.

Practicing patience and persistence:

11. Bouncing back from setbacks and disappointments requires patience and persistence. It is important to understand that progress takes time and setbacks are not indicative of failure. By staying committed to their goals and persevering through challenges, individuals can overcome setbacks and ultimately achieve success.

Learning and growing:

12. Every setback and disappointment presents an opportunity for learning and growth. It is essential to reflect on the experience and identify the lessons and insights gained. By embracing a mindset of continuous learning, individuals can extract wisdom from setbacks and apply it to future endeavors, increasing their resilience and improving their chances of success.

Celebrating small victories:

13.While setbacks and disappointments may overshadow progress, it is important to celebrate small victories along the way. Recognizing and acknowledging even the smallest accomplishments can boost confidence and motivation. By celebrating progress, individuals maintain a positive outlook and are better equipped to handle setbacks.

Cultivating a supportive environment:

14.Surrounding oneself with a supportive environment can significantly impact the ability to bounce back from setbacks and disappointments. Building a network of individuals who believe in and encourage personal growth provides invaluable support. Engaging with like-minded individuals, joining support groups, or seeking mentorship can offer guidance and inspiration during challenging times.

Maintaining a long-term perspective:

15.Setbacks and disappointments are temporary roadblocks on the journey towards success. It is important to maintain a long-term perspective and recognize that setbacks do not define one's potential or future outcomes. By viewing setbacks as mere detours, individuals can stay focused on their goals and keep moving forward.

Conclusion:

Chapter 38 explores the art of bouncing back from setbacks and disappointments. By cultivating resilience, embracing a growth mindset, managing emotions effectively, seeking support, learning from failure, and practicing self-compassion, individuals can navigate through challenges with grace and determination. Setbacks and disappointments are inevitable, but with the right mindset and strategies, individuals can bounce back stronger and continue their journey towards personal and professional success.

Chapter 39: Using mistakes as learning opportunities.

―――――

Introduction:

Chapter 39 explores the concept of using mistakes as valuable learning opportunities. Mistakes are a natural part of life, and instead of viewing them as failures, this chapter encourages individuals to shift their perspective and see them as stepping stones to growth and improvement. By embracing mistakes and adopting a mindset of continuous learning, individuals can extract valuable lessons, develop resilience, and achieve greater success in their personal and professional lives.

Embracing a growth mindset:

1.Using mistakes as learning opportunities starts with embracing a growth mindset. This mindset believes that intelligence, abilities, and skills can be developed through dedication, effort, and learning from experiences. By viewing mistakes as opportunities for growth rather than signs of incompetence, individuals open themselves up to valuable insights and personal development.

Normalizing mistakes:

2.Mistakes are an inherent part of the learning process. Normalizing mistakes creates a safe and supportive environment where individuals feel comfortable taking risks, trying new approaches, and learning from their errors. By recognizing that mistakes are a natural part of any journey, individuals can overcome the fear of failure and embrace a mindset focused on growth and improvement.

Analyzing and reflecting on mistakes:

3.To extract meaningful lessons from mistakes, it is important to analyze and reflect on them. This involves examining the factors that contributed to the mistake, identifying patterns or recurring errors, and understanding the underlying causes. By engaging in self-reflection and honest evaluation, individuals gain insights into their behaviors, decision-making processes, and areas for improvement.

Taking responsibility:

4.Taking responsibility for mistakes is a crucial step in using them as learning opportunities. Acknowledging one's role in the mistake and accepting accountability fosters personal growth and allows for constructive learning. By taking ownership of mistakes, individuals can develop self-awareness, learn from their actions, and make the necessary changes to avoid similar errors in the future.

Extracting lessons and applying knowledge:

5.Mistakes provide valuable lessons and insights that can be applied to future situations. By identifying the specific lessons learned from each mistake, individuals can develop strategies, refine their approaches, and make better-informed decisions. This iterative process of learning from mistakes helps individuals to continuously improve and increase their chances of success.

Seeking feedback:

6.Feedback from others is a valuable resource when learning from mistakes. Seeking feedback allows individuals to gain different perspectives, identify blind spots, and receive constructive criticism. By actively seeking feedback, individuals can gain valuable insights into their strengths and areas for growth, enabling them to make necessary adjustments and improve their performance.

Experimenting and taking calculated risks:

7.Using mistakes as learning opportunities involves embracing experimentation and taking calculated risks. It requires stepping outside of one's comfort zone and being open to the possibility of making mistakes. By taking calculated risks, individuals expand their knowledge, gain new experiences, and discover innovative solutions. Even if mistakes occur, the lessons learned contribute to personal and professional growth.

Cultivating a supportive environment:

8.Creating a supportive environment is essential when using mistakes as learning opportunities. Surrounding oneself with supportive individuals who encourage learning from mistakes fosters a positive mindset and growth-oriented culture. Sharing experiences, discussing lessons learned, and providing support and encouragement create an environment conducive to personal development and continuous improvement.

Embracing failure as a stepping stone to success:

9.Failure is often seen as a negative outcome, but it can be a powerful catalyst for growth and success. Embracing failure as a stepping stone to success involves reframing setbacks and failures as opportunities to learn, adapt, and grow. By shifting the perspective from failure as a final outcome to a temporary setback, individuals develop resilience, determination, and the ability to bounce back stronger than before.

Applying continuous improvement:

10.Using mistakes as learning opportunities involves applying continuous improvement principles. Continuous improvement is the process of making incremental changes and adjustments based on lessons learned from mistakes and past experiences. It emphasizes the importance of constantly evaluating and refining one's approach to achieve better outcomes. By embracing continuous improvement, individuals demonstrate a commitment to personal growth and development.

Developing problem-solving skills:

11.Mistakes often present unique challenges that require problem-solving skills. When individuals encounter a mistake, they have an opportunity to analyze the situation, identify the root causes, and develop effective solutions. By honing their problem-solving skills, individuals become more adept at handling setbacks, finding creative solutions, and preventing similar mistakes in the future.

Cultivating resilience and persistence:

12.Using mistakes as learning opportunities requires resilience and persistence. It is essential to bounce back from setbacks, learn from mistakes, and keep moving forward. Resilience allows individuals to maintain a positive attitude, adapt to change, and persevere through challenges. By cultivating resilience and persistence, individuals develop the strength to overcome obstacles and achieve their goals.

Embracing a culture of learning:

13.In organizations and communities, fostering a culture of learning is essential for using mistakes as learning opportunities. This involves promoting a growth mindset, encouraging continuous learning and improvement, and celebrating the lessons gained from mistakes. By creating a culture that values learning and embraces mistakes as part of the journey, individuals feel empowered to take risks, innovate, and learn from their experiences.

Applying feedback loops:

14.Feedback loops are an effective tool for using mistakes as learning opportunities. Establishing feedback mechanisms allows individuals to receive timely and constructive feedback on their performance and areas for improvement. By incorporating feedback loops into their personal and professional lives, individuals can gain valuable insights, make adjustments, and continuously enhance their skills and abilities.

Embracing a learning orientation:

15.A learning orientation involves seeking knowledge, seeking feedback, and continuously improving oneself. It requires a mindset that values growth, curiosity, and self-reflection. By adopting a learning orientation, individuals shift their focus from the fear of making mistakes to the excitement of learning and growing. This mindset enables them to embrace mistakes as valuable opportunities for personal and professional development.

Conclusion:

Chapter 39 delves into the concept of using mistakes as learning opportunities. By embracing a growth mindset, normalizing mistakes, analyzing and reflecting on mistakes, taking responsibility, extracting lessons, seeking feedback, and embracing failure as a stepping stone to success, individuals can harness the power of mistakes to fuel their personal growth and development. By viewing mistakes as valuable learning experiences and applying the lessons learned, individuals can continuously improve, achieve greater success, and lead more fulfilling lives.

Chapter 40: Cultivating perseverance and endurance.

―――

I ntroduction:

Chapter 40 explores the importance of cultivating perseverance and endurance in the pursuit of personal growth and success. Perseverance is the ability to persist in the face of challenges, setbacks, and obstacles, while endurance refers to the ability to sustain effort over an extended period. Together, these qualities empower individuals to overcome adversity, maintain focus, and achieve their goals. This chapter provides insights and strategies for developing and nurturing perseverance and endurance in various aspects of life.

Understanding the power of perseverance:

1.Perseverance is a key ingredient for success. It involves maintaining determination and persistence, even in the face of difficulties and disappointments. By recognizing that challenges are a natural part of any journey, individuals can develop the resilience and tenacity needed to navigate obstacles and stay committed to their goals.

Setting clear and meaningful goals:

2.Having clear and meaningful goals provides a sense of direction and purpose, which fuels perseverance and endurance. When individuals have a compelling vision of what they want to achieve, they are more likely to stay motivated and push through obstacles. Setting specific, measurable, achievable, relevant, and time-bound

(SMART) goals helps individuals track their progress and stay focused on the desired outcome.

Developing a positive mindset:

3.A positive mindset plays a crucial role in cultivating perseverance and endurance. By adopting a positive outlook, individuals can reframe challenges as opportunities for growth, maintain optimism in the face of setbacks, and stay motivated to overcome obstacles. Positive self-talk, gratitude practices, and visualization techniques are effective strategies for fostering a positive mindset.

Building resilience:

4.Resilience is closely linked to perseverance and endurance. It is the ability to bounce back from adversity and maintain mental and emotional strength. Building resilience involves developing coping mechanisms, such as stress management techniques, seeking support from others, and practicing self-care. By enhancing resilience, individuals can better navigate challenges and sustain their efforts over time.

Breaking goals into manageable steps:

5.Long-term goals can be overwhelming, making it challenging to maintain perseverance and endurance. Breaking goals into smaller, manageable steps creates a sense of progress and accomplishment along the way. By focusing on one step at a time, individuals can maintain motivation, stay engaged, and build momentum towards their desired outcomes.

Developing grit:

6.Grit is a combination of passion and perseverance for long-term goals. It is the willingness to put in sustained effort and endure hardships to achieve success. Developing grit involves cultivating a growth mindset, maintaining a long-term perspective, embracing failure as an opportunity to learn, and staying committed to the pursuit of excellence.

Seeking support and accountability:

7.Having a support system and accountability measures in place can greatly enhance perseverance and endurance. Surrounding oneself with supportive individuals who believe in their goals and provide encouragement and guidance can help individuals stay motivated during challenging times. Additionally, accountability partners or groups can provide the necessary structure and motivation to keep individuals on track.

Practicing self-reflection:

8.Self-reflection is a powerful tool for cultivating perseverance and endurance. By regularly reflecting on progress, setbacks, and lessons learned, individuals can adjust their strategies, identify areas for improvement, and stay aligned with their goals. Self-reflection enhances self-awareness and helps individuals stay resilient and focused on their long-term vision.

Developing a growth mindset:

9.A growth mindset is essential for cultivating perseverance and endurance. It is the belief that abilities and intelligence can be developed through dedication, effort, and continuous learning. By embracing challenges, viewing failure as a learning opportunity, and persistently seeking improvement, individuals with a growth mindset are better equipped to handle setbacks and stay motivated.

Celebrating milestones and progress:

10.Celebrating milestones and progress along the journey provides a sense of accomplishment and boosts motivation. Recognizing and acknowledging small victories along the way can help individuals maintain their perseverance and endurance. Celebrating milestones can take various forms, such as rewarding oneself, sharing achievements with others, or reflecting on the progress made. These celebrations serve as reminders of the hard work and dedication invested, reinforcing the commitment to continue moving forward.

Developing emotional resilience:

11.Emotional resilience is the ability to manage and bounce back from emotional challenges and setbacks. It involves recognizing and regulating emotions, practicing self-care, and developing healthy coping mechanisms. By strengthening emotional resilience, individuals can navigate difficult situations without becoming overwhelmed or giving up, thereby maintaining their perseverance and endurance.

Embracing failure as a learning opportunity:

12.Failure is an inevitable part of any journey towards personal growth and success. Rather than seeing failure as a setback, individuals can reframe it as a valuable learning opportunity. Embracing failure allows individuals to extract lessons, adjust their approach, and grow stronger. By viewing failure as a stepping stone towards success, individuals are more likely to persevere and endure through challenging times.

Cultivating patience:

13.Patience is a vital attribute in developing perseverance and endurance. It involves accepting that progress takes time and understanding that setbacks and obstacles are part of the process. Cultivating patience allows individuals to stay focused and committed to their goals, even when the desired outcomes take longer to materialize. Patience helps individuals maintain a long-term perspective and resist the temptation to give up prematurely.

Maintaining a healthy work-life balance:

14.Balancing work and personal life is essential for sustaining perseverance and endurance. Overworking and neglecting personal needs can lead to burnout and diminish motivation. By prioritizing self-care, setting boundaries, and allocating time for rest and rejuvenation, individuals can replenish their energy and maintain their drive to persevere towards their goals.

Seeking inspiration and learning from others:

15.Drawing inspiration from others who have demonstrated perseverance and endurance can fuel one's own determination. Learning from their stories, strategies, and experiences can provide valuable insights and motivation. Whether through books, podcasts, mentors, or role models, seeking inspiration from others who have overcome challenges and achieved success can help individuals stay motivated and resilient.

Conclusion:

Chapter 40 explores the significance of cultivating perseverance and endurance in the pursuit of personal growth and success. By understanding the power of perseverance, setting clear goals, maintaining a positive mindset, building resilience, breaking goals into manageable steps, developing grit, seeking support, practicing self-reflection, embracing failure as a learning opportunity, and cultivating patience, individuals can foster the qualities necessary to overcome obstacles, stay motivated, and achieve their long-term goals. By embodying perseverance and endurance, individuals can navigate challenges, maintain focus, and ultimately realize their full potential.

Chapter 41: Finding personal purpose and passion.

———

I ntroduction:

Chapter 41 explores the profound importance of finding personal purpose and passion in life. Discovering one's purpose and embracing passion not only brings a sense of fulfillment and joy, but it also fuels motivation, resilience, and the drive to create a meaningful impact in the world. This chapter delves into the process of self-exploration, uncovering core values, aligning with passions, and taking steps towards living a purpose-driven life.

Understanding the significance of personal purpose:

1.Personal purpose gives life meaning and direction. It is the deep-seated reason behind one's existence and the driving force behind their actions and choices. By understanding their purpose, individuals gain a sense of clarity and focus, enabling them to make decisions aligned with their values and passions.

Engaging in self-reflection:

2.Self-reflection is a crucial step in the journey of finding personal purpose and passion. It involves introspection, exploring one's values, strengths, interests, and aspirations. By examining past experiences, identifying patterns, and reflecting on what brings a sense of fulfillment, individuals can gain insights into their authentic selves and discover their unique purpose.

Clarifying core values:

3.Core values serve as guiding principles that define what is most important to individuals. By identifying and clarifying their core values, individuals can align their actions and decisions with what truly matters to them. Core values provide a compass for making choices that are in line with one's authentic self and contribute to a sense of purpose.

Exploring passions and interests:

4.Passions and interests are the fuel that ignites personal purpose. By exploring different activities, hobbies, and subjects, individuals can uncover what brings them joy, excitement, and a sense of fulfillment. Engaging in activities that align with their passions allows individuals to tap into their unique talents and create a life that is meaningful to them.

Seeking meaningful work:

5.Finding personal purpose and passion often involves aligning one's professional life with their values and interests. Individuals are encouraged to explore careers or pursuits that resonate with their passions and provide a sense of purpose. When work is aligned with personal values, individuals experience a deep sense of satisfaction and motivation, leading to greater fulfillment in their professional lives.

Embracing personal growth and development:

6.Personal purpose and passion are not static; they evolve over time. Embracing personal growth and development is essential in the journey of discovering and living one's purpose. This involves seeking opportunities for learning, expanding skills, and stepping out of comfort zones. Personal growth fuels passion, as individuals continuously evolve and refine their sense of purpose.

Overcoming fear and resistance:

7.Finding personal purpose and passion can be a transformative process that involves stepping outside of one's comfort zone and confronting fears and resistance. Fear of failure, societal expectations, or judgment can hinder individuals from fully embracing their purpose. By acknowledging and addressing these fears, individuals can break free from limiting beliefs and pursue their passions with courage and determination.

Taking action:

8.Discovering personal purpose and passion is not enough; action is required to bring them to life. Taking small steps towards aligning daily actions with one's purpose is essential. It may involve setting goals, creating action plans, and making intentional choices that reflect one's values and passions. Taking action reinforces commitment, builds momentum, and propels individuals closer to living a purpose-driven life.

Cultivating gratitude and mindfulness:

9.Gratitude and mindfulness are powerful practices that enhance the experience of personal purpose and passion. By cultivating gratitude for the present moment and appreciating the journey towards finding purpose, individuals develop a deeper sense of fulfillment and contentment. Mindfulness allows individuals to fully engage in activities aligned with their purpose, savoring the experience and finding joy in the process.

Making a positive impact:

10.Personal purpose and passion often extend beyond individual fulfillment; they involve making a positive impact on others and the world. When individuals align their purpose with service to others, they find a deeper sense of meaning and fulfillment. This can be achieved through acts of kindness, volunteering, advocating for causes, or pursuing careers that contribute to the well-being of others.

Nurturing relationships:

11.Finding personal purpose and passion is not a solitary journey. Nurturing meaningful relationships plays a vital role in the process. Surrounding oneself with supportive individuals who share similar values and passions can provide encouragement, inspiration, and opportunities for collaboration. Building a network of like-minded individuals fosters a sense of community and reinforces one's commitment to living a purpose-driven life.

Embracing growth and adaptability:

12.As individuals uncover their personal purpose and passion, it is important to embrace growth and adaptability. Purpose and passions may evolve over time, and individuals need to be open to new opportunities and experiences. By remaining flexible and adaptable, individuals can navigate changes and challenges while staying true to their core values and overarching purpose.

Fostering self-compassion:

13.The journey of finding personal purpose and passion can sometimes be challenging and accompanied by setbacks and self-doubt. Fostering self-compassion is crucial during these times. By practicing self-care, embracing imperfections, and treating oneself with kindness and understanding, individuals can cultivate resilience and maintain a positive mindset throughout their journey.

Continuous reflection and refinement:

14.Discovering personal purpose and passion is not a one-time event; it is an ongoing process. Regular reflection and refinement are necessary to stay connected to one's purpose and ensure alignment with changing values and circumstances. By periodically reassessing goals, values, and passions, individuals can make adjustments and continue to grow and evolve in their pursuit of a purpose-driven life.

Conclusion:

Chapter 41 highlights the significance of finding personal purpose and passion in life. By engaging in self-reflection, clarifying core values, exploring passions and interests, seeking meaningful work, embracing personal growth, overcoming fear and resistance, taking action, cultivating gratitude and mindfulness, making a positive impact, nurturing relationships, embracing growth and adaptability, fostering self-compassion, and engaging in continuous reflection and refinement, individuals can uncover their unique purpose and live a more fulfilling and meaningful life. Finding personal purpose and passion empowers individuals to create a positive impact, find joy, and experience a deep sense of fulfillment as they align their actions and choices with their authentic selves.

Chapter 42: Cultivating a positive attitude.

———

Introduction:

Chapter 42 explores the transformative power of cultivating a positive attitude in every aspect of life. A positive attitude is a mindset that focuses on optimism, resilience, and finding the silver lining in any situation. This chapter delves into the importance of cultivating a positive attitude, strategies to shift negative thinking patterns, and the benefits of maintaining a positive outlook on life.

Understanding the power of attitude:

> 1.Attitude is a choice that significantly influences how we perceive and respond to the world around us. A positive attitude enables us to approach challenges with optimism, embrace change with resilience, and maintain a hopeful outlook even in difficult times. It shapes our thoughts, emotions, and actions, ultimately impacting our overall well-being and success.

Recognizing negative thinking patterns:

> 2.Negative thinking patterns, such as pessimism, self-doubt, and self-criticism, can hinder personal growth and hinder happiness. By becoming aware of these patterns, individuals can start to challenge and replace them with more positive and empowering thoughts. Recognizing negative thinking allows for the intentional cultivation of a positive attitude.

Practicing gratitude:

3.Gratitude is a powerful tool for cultivating a positive attitude. By focusing on the blessings and positive aspects of life, individuals shift their attention away from negativity and develop a sense of appreciation. Regular gratitude practice, such as keeping a gratitude journal or expressing gratitude to others, fosters a positive mindset and enhances overall well-being.

Reframing challenges:

4.A positive attitude involves reframing challenges as opportunities for growth and learning. Instead of viewing setbacks as failures, individuals with a positive attitude see them as valuable lessons that contribute to personal development. By reframing challenges, individuals can approach them with a proactive and solution-oriented mindset, increasing their chances of success.

Surrounding yourself with positivity:

5.The company we keep significantly influences our attitude and mindset. Surrounding ourselves with positive, supportive, and uplifting individuals creates an environment that fosters a positive attitude. Seek out relationships with people who inspire, motivate, and encourage personal growth. Their positivity will reinforce your own optimistic outlook.

Practicing self-compassion:

6.Self-compassion is a key aspect of cultivating a positive attitude. It involves treating oneself with kindness, understanding, and acceptance, especially during times of difficulty or failure. By practicing self-compassion, individuals develop resilience and bounce back from setbacks with a renewed sense of optimism and self-belief.

Embracing optimism:

7.Optimism is a core component of a positive attitude. It is the belief that favorable outcomes are possible and that setbacks are temporary. Embracing optimism allows individuals to approach challenges with confidence and perseverance, fueling their motivation to overcome obstacles and achieve their goals.

Practicing positive self-talk:

8.The language we use towards ourselves influences our attitude and self-perception. By practicing positive self-talk, individuals replace negative and self-limiting beliefs with empowering and affirming statements. This shift in self-dialogue fosters a positive attitude and strengthens self-confidence.

Cultivating resilience:

9.Resilience is the ability to bounce back from adversity and maintain a positive attitude in the face of challenges. Cultivating resilience involves developing coping mechanisms, seeking support when needed, and maintaining a growth mindset. Resilient individuals view setbacks as temporary and see them as opportunities for personal growth.

Focusing on solutions:

10.A positive attitude directs our focus towards finding solutions rather than dwelling on problems. Instead of getting caught up in negativity, individuals with a positive attitude seek proactive approaches to resolve challenges. By focusing on solutions, they maintain a positive mindset and take action towards achieving their desired outcomes.

Embracing positivity in communication:

11.Communication plays a vital role in cultivating a positive attitude. By embracing positivity in communication, individuals can foster a harmonious and uplifting environment. This involves using encouraging and supportive language, actively listening to others, and offering constructive feedback. Positive communication enhances relationships, promotes understanding, and contributes to a positive overall atmosphere.

Finding joy in the present moment:

12.A positive attitude involves finding joy in the present moment and appreciating the simple pleasures of life. By practicing mindfulness and being fully present, individuals can cultivate a sense of gratitude and contentment. This allows them to let go of worries about the past or future and focus on the beauty and opportunities that exist in the present.

Seeking growth and learning opportunities:

13.A positive attitude encourages a mindset of continuous growth and learning. Embracing new challenges and seeking opportunities to expand knowledge and skills not only enhances personal development but also reinforces a positive outlook. By embracing a growth mindset, individuals approach life with curiosity, resilience, and enthusiasm.

Celebrating successes, big and small:

14.Recognizing and celebrating successes, no matter how small, is an important aspect of cultivating a positive attitude. Acknowledging achievements boosts self-confidence, reinforces a positive self-image, and provides motivation to continue working towards goals. By celebrating milestones along the journey, individuals maintain a positive mindset and fuel their drive for further growth.

Cultivating optimistic thinking:

15.Optimistic thinking is a key component of a positive attitude. It involves consciously choosing to see the bright side of situations, even in the face of adversity. By reframing challenges, focusing on solutions, and maintaining a belief in a favorable outcome, individuals cultivate an optimistic mindset that fuels their resilience and determination.

Practicing self-care:

16.Taking care of oneself physically, mentally, and emotionally is essential for cultivating a positive attitude. Engaging in self-care activities, such as exercise, adequate rest, healthy eating, and engaging in hobbies, replenishes energy, reduces stress, and promotes overall well-being. By prioritizing self-care, individuals are better equipped to maintain a positive attitude and handle life's challenges.

Embracing a growth mindset:

17. A growth mindset is the belief that abilities and intelligence can be developed through dedication and effort. By embracing a growth mindset, individuals view challenges as opportunities for learning and growth rather than as limitations. This mindset fosters a positive attitude by empowering individuals to embrace challenges, persist in the face of setbacks, and continuously improve themselves.

Cultivating resilient thinking:

18. Resilient thinking involves reframing negative or stressful situations in a way that promotes resilience and a positive attitude. By focusing on strengths, seeking lessons, and maintaining a belief in one's ability to overcome obstacles, individuals develop a resilient mindset. This resilient thinking enables individuals to navigate challenges with optimism and adaptability.

Conclusion:

Chapter 42 emphasizes the importance of cultivating a positive attitude as a catalyst for personal growth, resilience, and overall well-being. By understanding the power of attitude, recognizing negative thinking patterns, practicing gratitude, reframing challenges, surrounding oneself with positivity, practicing self-compassion, embracing optimism, using positive self-talk, cultivating resilience, focusing on solutions, embracing positivity in communication, finding joy in the present moment, seeking growth and learning opportunities, celebrating successes, cultivating optimistic thinking, practicing self-care, embracing a growth mindset, and cultivating resilient thinking, individuals can foster a positive attitude that enriches their lives and the lives of those around them. With a positive attitude, individuals can overcome obstacles, embrace opportunities, and create a more fulfilling and meaningful existence.

Chapter 43: Achieving work-life balance.

Introduction:

In today's fast-paced and demanding world, achieving a healthy work-life balance has become a significant challenge for many individuals. Juggling career responsibilities, personal commitments, and self-care can often feel overwhelming. However, finding a harmonious equilibrium between work and personal life is essential for overall well-being and fulfillment. In this chapter, we will explore strategies and practices that can help individuals achieve a better work-life balance and create a more satisfying and meaningful life.

Defining work-life balance:

1.Work-life balance refers to the equilibrium between an individual's professional and personal life domains. It involves allocating time, energy, and attention to work-related tasks, personal relationships, self-care, and leisure activities in a manner that satisfies individual needs and priorities. Achieving work-life balance is about finding a sustainable rhythm that allows individuals to thrive in both their professional and personal realms.

Assessing priorities and values:

2.The first step towards achieving work-life balance is to assess priorities and values. Individuals must identify what truly matters to them and align their actions and commitments accordingly. This involves clarifying personal and professional goals, determining core values, and making conscious choices that support their priorities. By gaining clarity on what is truly important, individuals can make informed decisions and allocate their time and resources accordingly.

Setting boundaries:

3.Setting clear boundaries between work and personal life is crucial for achieving work-life balance. This means defining specific work hours and sticking to them, avoiding overcommitment, and learning to say no when necessary. Establishing boundaries allows individuals to protect their personal time, maintain healthy relationships, and prevent burnout. It also enables individuals to be fully present and engaged in both their work and personal life domains.

Effective time management:

4.Mastering the art of time management is essential for achieving work-life balance. This involves prioritizing tasks, setting realistic deadlines, and creating a structured schedule that allows for dedicated time for work, personal activities, and self-care. Effective time management helps individuals maximize productivity, reduce stress, and create space for leisure and relaxation. By being intentional with their time, individuals can ensure that both work and personal commitments are met without sacrificing their well-being.

Building supportive relationships:

5.Nurturing supportive relationships is crucial for achieving work-life balance. This includes fostering open communication with colleagues, supervisors, and loved ones, as well as seeking assistance when needed. Building a strong support network helps individuals share responsibilities, delegate tasks, and create a sense of community. Having supportive relationships allows individuals to lean on others during challenging times and enhances overall well-being.

Prioritizing self-care:

6.Self-care is a fundamental aspect of achieving work-life balance. Taking care of one's physical, mental, and emotional well-being is essential for maintaining productivity, reducing stress, and enhancing overall happiness. This includes engaging in activities that promote relaxation, exercise, healthy eating, and adequate rest. Prioritizing self-care allows individuals to recharge, replenish their energy, and approach both work and personal life with renewed vigor.

Flexibility and adaptability:

7.In today's dynamic work environment, flexibility and adaptability are key to achieving work-life balance. Embracing flexible work arrangements, such as remote work or flexible hours, can provide individuals with greater control over their schedules. Additionally, cultivating adaptability helps individuals navigate unexpected changes and challenges with resilience and ease. Being open to new approaches and adjusting priorities when necessary allows individuals to maintain equilibrium and minimize stress.

Creating rituals and boundaries:

8.Establishing rituals and boundaries can contribute to a better work-life balance. Rituals can be daily, weekly, or monthly practices that help individuals transition between work and personal life, such as creating a morning routine or setting aside dedicated family time. Boundaries can include setting aside specific days or times for personal activities and avoiding work-related tasks during those periods. By incorporating rituals and boundaries into their lives, individuals can create a sense of structure and separation between work and personal life, promoting a healthier balance.

Embracing mindfulness:

9.Practicing mindfulness can significantly contribute to achieving work-life balance. Mindfulness involves being fully present and engaged in the present moment, without judgment or attachment. By cultivating mindfulness, individuals can better manage stress, improve focus and concentration, and enhance overall well-being. Mindful practices such as meditation, deep breathing exercises, or taking mindful breaks throughout the day can help individuals find inner calm amidst the demands of work and personal life.

Continual evaluation and adjustments:

10.Achieving work-life balance is an ongoing process that requires continual evaluation and adjustments. As priorities, circumstances, and responsibilities evolve, it is essential to regularly assess and reassess how well one's work-life balance is being maintained. This may involve reevaluating goals, reassessing time commitments, and making necessary changes to restore balance. It is important to remember that work-life balance is not a one-time achievement but a continuous journey of self-awareness and adaptation.

Conclusion:

Striving for work-life balance is a vital endeavor that enables individuals to lead fulfilling and meaningful lives. By implementing strategies such as setting boundaries, effective time management, nurturing supportive relationships, prioritizing self-care, and embracing flexibility, individuals can find a harmonious integration of work and personal life. Remember, achieving work-life balance is a personal and individualized process, and it may look different for everyone. The key is to prioritize what truly matters, make conscious choices, and regularly evaluate and adjust to maintain a healthy and fulfilling equilibrium. By doing so, individuals can experience increased happiness, reduced stress, and a greater sense of overall well-being in both their professional and personal endeavors.

Chapter 44: Nurturing relationships and social engagement.

_____

I ntroduction:

Human beings are social creatures by nature, and nurturing meaningful relationships is essential for our overall well-being and happiness. In this chapter, we will explore the importance of nurturing relationships and social engagement in our lives. We will discuss strategies and practices that can help individuals develop and maintain healthy connections, foster deeper bonds, and create a sense of belonging in their personal and professional spheres.

The significance of relationships:

> 1.Strong and supportive relationships play a vital role in our lives. They provide us with emotional support, companionship, and a sense of belonging. Healthy relationships contribute to our mental and physical well-being, enhance our resilience, and provide opportunities for personal growth and fulfillment. Nurturing relationships is a lifelong endeavor that requires time, effort, and genuine care.

Cultivating authentic connections:

> 2.Building authentic connections requires openness, vulnerability, and genuine interest in others. It involves being present, actively listening, and showing empathy. Cultivating authentic relationships means being yourself and allowing others to do the same. By fostering trust and

understanding, individuals can create a safe space for meaningful connections to flourish.

Investing time and effort:

3.Nurturing relationships requires a conscious investment of time and effort. It involves prioritizing quality interactions, making time for regular communication, and engaging in shared activities. This may include scheduling regular meet-ups, phone calls, or video chats, participating in group activities or hobbies, and celebrating milestones and achievements together. By allocating dedicated time for relationships, individuals can strengthen the bonds they share with others.

Effective communication:

4.Effective communication is essential for nurturing relationships. It involves not only expressing oneself clearly but also actively listening to others and seeking to understand their perspectives. Good communication involves honesty, respect, and compassion. It is important to communicate openly, share thoughts and feelings, and address conflicts or misunderstandings in a constructive and empathetic manner.

Building trust and respect:

5.Trust and respect are the foundation of any healthy relationship. Individuals can build trust by being reliable, keeping commitments, and being honest and transparent. Respect is shown by valuing others' opinions, boundaries, and autonomy. By fostering trust and respect, individuals can create a safe and supportive environment for meaningful connections to thrive.

Balancing independence and interdependence:

6.Nurturing relationships requires finding a balance between independence and interdependence. While it is important to maintain a sense of self and individuality, it is equally crucial to recognize the value of interdependence and mutual support. Balancing these aspects allows individuals to foster healthy relationships that promote personal growth, shared experiences, and a sense of community.

Diverse relationships:

7.Nurturing relationships goes beyond family and close friends. It also involves cultivating diverse connections with colleagues, mentors, community members, and individuals from different backgrounds and cultures. Embracing diversity in relationships exposes individuals to new perspectives, broadens their horizons, and fosters a greater understanding and appreciation of others.

Social engagement and community involvement:

8.Being socially engaged and involved in the community has numerous benefits for personal well-being and relationship-building. Engaging in community activities, volunteering, or joining clubs and organizations allows individuals to connect with like-minded people, contribute to causes they care about, and expand their social networks. Social engagement not only enriches individual lives but also strengthens the fabric of the community.

Balancing virtual and in-person connections:

9.In today's digital age, nurturing relationships involves finding a balance between virtual and in-person connections. While technology allows us to connect with others across distances, it is important to prioritize face-to-face interactions whenever possible. In-person interactions foster deeper emotional connections, non-verbal communication, and a sense of presence that cannot be fully replicated through virtual means.

Self-reflection and growth:

10.Self-reflection plays a crucial role in nurturing relationships and social engagement. Taking the time to reflect on our own thoughts, emotions, and behaviors allows us to gain insights into how we relate to others and identify areas for personal growth. By practicing self-awareness, individuals can develop a deeper understanding of their strengths, weaknesses, and patterns of behavior that may impact their relationships. Self-reflection also helps individuals recognize and address any negative or harmful patterns that may hinder their ability to build and maintain healthy connections.

Resolving conflict and building resilience:

11.Conflict is a natural part of any relationship, and learning how to effectively resolve conflicts is essential for nurturing healthy connections. Conflict resolution involves open communication, active listening, and a willingness to find mutually agreeable solutions. It also requires empathy, understanding, and the ability to forgive and move forward. By addressing conflicts with respect and resilience, individuals can strengthen their relationships and foster a greater sense of trust and understanding.

The power of gratitude and appreciation:

12.Expressing gratitude and appreciation is a powerful way to nurture relationships. Taking the time to acknowledge and recognize the positive qualities and contributions of others strengthens the bonds we share. Expressing gratitude not only fosters a positive atmosphere but also helps individuals feel valued and appreciated, leading to deeper connections and a greater sense of well-being within the relationship.

Boundaries and self-care:

13.Nurturing relationships also involves setting healthy boundaries and prioritizing self-care. It is essential to establish clear boundaries that protect our physical, emotional, and mental well-being. By communicating our needs and limits effectively, we create an environment of mutual respect and understanding. Additionally, practicing self-care ensures that we have the energy and capacity to engage in relationships authentically and sustainably.

Seeking support and building a supportive network:

14.Nurturing relationships includes recognizing when we need support and reaching out to others. Building a supportive network of individuals who uplift, inspire, and encourage us is vital for our well-being. Seeking support from trusted friends, family members, or professional networks helps us navigate challenges, gain perspective, and find solace during difficult times.

Continuous growth and adaptation:

15.Nurturing relationships is an ongoing process that requires continuous growth and adaptation. As individuals and circumstances change, relationships also evolve. It is important to remain open to learning, growing, and adapting our approach to relationships. By being flexible and willing to embrace new experiences and perspectives, we can strengthen our connections and foster a sense of growth together.

Conclusion:

Nurturing relationships and engaging socially are fundamental aspects of a fulfilling and meaningful life. By investing time, effort, and genuine care into our relationships, we cultivate a supportive network of connections that enrich our lives and contribute to our overall well-being. Through effective communication, building trust, embracing diversity, and practicing self-reflection, we can foster deep and meaningful connections with others. Remember, nurturing relationships is an ongoing journey that requires continuous effort, but the rewards are immeasurable – deeper connections, increased happiness, and a sense of belonging and purpose in our lives.

Chapter 45: The power of gratitude and mindfulness.

I ntroduction:

In a fast-paced and often stressful world, cultivating gratitude and mindfulness can have a transformative effect on our lives. These practices allow us to shift our focus from what is lacking to what we already have, fostering a sense of contentment, joy, and fulfillment. In this chapter, we will explore the power of gratitude and mindfulness and how they can positively impact our well-being and relationships.

1.The essence of gratitude:

Gratitude is a state of appreciation and thankfulness for the blessings, experiences, and people in our lives. It is about recognizing the positive aspects and expressing genuine appreciation for them. Gratitude shifts our perspective from scarcity to abundance, reminding us of the many blessings that surround us every day. By cultivating gratitude, we enhance our overall well-being and develop a more positive outlook on life.

2.The benefits of gratitude:

Practicing gratitude has numerous benefits for our physical, mental, and emotional well-being. Research has shown that regularly expressing gratitude can reduce stress, improve sleep quality, boost immune function, and increase overall happiness. Gratitude also enhances our relationships by fostering a sense of connection, empathy, and kindness. When we express gratitude to others, it strengthens our bonds and deepens our connections.

3.Cultivating a gratitude practice:

Developing a gratitude practice involves consciously incorporating gratitude into our daily lives. This can be done through simple exercises such as keeping a gratitude journal, where we write down three things we are grateful for each day. Another approach is to express gratitude directly to others through heartfelt thank-you notes or acts of kindness. By making gratitude a habit, we train our minds to notice and appreciate the positive aspects of our lives.

4.The art of mindfulness:

Mindfulness is the practice of being fully present in the moment, without judgment or attachment. It involves paying attention to our thoughts, feelings, and sensations in a non-reactive manner. Mindfulness allows us to cultivate a greater sense of self-awareness and to observe our experiences without getting caught up in them. By practicing mindfulness, we can reduce stress, enhance focus and concentration, and improve our overall well-being.

5.The benefits of mindfulness:

Mindfulness has been extensively studied and has shown significant benefits for our mental and physical health. Research has found that mindfulness reduces anxiety and depression, improves cognitive function, and promotes emotional regulation. It also enhances our relationships by improving communication and empathy. Mindfulness helps us cultivate a sense of inner calm and equanimity, allowing us to navigate life's challenges with greater resilience and clarity.

6.Incorporating mindfulness into daily life:

Integrating mindfulness into our daily lives can be done through various practices. Mindful meditation is a popular method that involves focusing on the breath or a specific sensation, allowing thoughts and emotions to come and go without judgment. Mindful eating, walking, and engaging in daily activities with full presence are other ways to bring mindfulness into our routines. By making mindfulness a part of our daily life, we can experience its transformative effects.

7.Gratitude and mindfulness in harmony:

Gratitude and mindfulness complement each other beautifully. When we practice gratitude, we become more aware of the present moment and the blessings it holds. Similarly, mindfulness allows us to appreciate and fully experience the gifts in our lives. By combining gratitude and mindfulness, we deepen our connection with the present moment and cultivate a profound sense of gratitude for the richness of life.

8.Applying gratitude and mindfulness in relationships:

Gratitude and mindfulness play a significant role in nurturing our relationships. When we cultivate gratitude, we become more aware of the positive qualities and actions of our loved ones, which strengthens our bond and appreciation for them. Mindfulness allows us to be fully present and attentive when we engage with others, listening deeply and responding with empathy. It helps us to truly understand and connect with their experiences, fostering trust and intimacy in our relationships. By practicing gratitude and mindfulness in our interactions, we create a positive and supportive environment that promotes open communication and mutual understanding.

9.Overcoming challenges with gratitude and mindfulness:

Gratitude and mindfulness can also help us navigate challenges and difficult times in our lives. When faced with adversity, practicing gratitude allows us to shift our focus to the things we still have, even amidst the difficulties. It helps us find silver linings and appreciate the lessons learned from challenging experiences. Mindfulness, on the other hand, enables us to stay present and non-judgmental, allowing us to respond to difficulties with clarity and resilience. By incorporating these practices, we can find strength and resilience in the face of adversity.

10.Daily rituals for gratitude and mindfulness:

To fully integrate gratitude and mindfulness into our lives, it is helpful to establish daily rituals. This could include starting each day with a gratitude reflection, expressing appreciation to loved ones, or incorporating mindfulness exercises into our routines. These rituals serve as anchors, reminding us to pause, reflect, and cultivate gratitude and mindfulness throughout the day. Consistency and commitment to these practices will deepen their impact on our well-being and personal growth.

Conclusion:

The power of gratitude and mindfulness cannot be overstated. They have the ability to transform our lives, enhance our well-being, and strengthen our relationships. By cultivating gratitude, we shift our perspective towards abundance and appreciate the richness of our lives. Mindfulness allows us to fully engage with the present moment and navigate life's challenges with grace and resilience. Together, gratitude and mindfulness create a powerful foundation for personal growth and a more fulfilling and meaningful life. Embrace the power of gratitude and mindfulness, and watch as they enrich every aspect of your life.

Chapter 46: Integrating lessons into daily life.

———

I ntroduction:

Learning and personal growth are continuous processes that extend beyond the pages of a book or the confines of a workshop. To truly benefit from the insights and lessons we acquire, it is essential to integrate them into our daily lives. In this chapter, we will explore strategies for effectively integrating the valuable lessons we learn into our daily routines and experiences.

1.Embracing a growth mindset:

Integrating lessons into daily life starts with adopting a growth mindset—an attitude that embraces learning, improvement, and the belief that our abilities can be developed through dedication and effort. By cultivating a growth mindset, we open ourselves to new possibilities and become more receptive to the lessons that come our way.

2.Reflecting on lessons:

Reflection is a powerful tool for integrating lessons into our lives. Taking the time to reflect on what we have learned allows us to deepen our understanding, make connections to our experiences, and identify practical ways to apply the lessons. Regular reflection can be done through journaling, meditation, or engaging in deep conversations with trusted individuals.

3.Setting actionable goals:

Once we have identified the lessons we want to integrate, setting actionable goals becomes crucial. By breaking down the lessons into tangible steps or actions, we create a roadmap for incorporating them into our daily lives. These goals should be specific, measurable, achievable, relevant, and time-bound (SMART), ensuring that we have a clear plan for implementation.

4.Creating daily rituals:

Daily rituals provide structure and consistency, making it easier to integrate lessons into our routines. Whether it's setting aside dedicated time for reflection, practicing gratitude, or engaging in specific activities related to the lessons, incorporating them into our daily rituals helps solidify their integration into our lives. Consistency is key to making these rituals a natural part of our day-to-day existence.

5.Practicing mindfulness:

Mindfulness plays a vital role in integrating lessons into daily life. By cultivating present-moment awareness, we can consciously apply the lessons we have learned to our thoughts, actions, and interactions. Mindfulness helps us stay attuned to our values, make conscious choices, and respond in ways that align with our personal growth goals. Regular mindfulness practices such as meditation or mindful breathing can support this integration process.

6.Seeking accountability and support:

Integrating lessons into daily life can be challenging without accountability and support. Sharing our goals and progress with trusted friends, mentors, or accountability partners can provide valuable encouragement, feedback, and motivation. Collaborating with others who share similar growth aspirations can also create a supportive community that reinforces our commitment to integrating the lessons.

7.Embracing iteration and adaptation:

Integrating lessons is an ongoing process that requires flexibility and adaptability. It's important to recognize that our understanding and application of lessons may evolve over time. Embracing a mindset of iteration allows us to continuously refine our approach, learn from our experiences, and make necessary adjustments along the way. It's okay to experiment, make mistakes, and adapt as we strive to integrate the lessons into our lives.

8.Celebrating progress:

Celebrating milestones and progress is crucial in the integration process. Recognizing and acknowledging the positive changes and growth we have experienced reinforces our commitment and motivation. Celebrating milestones also serves as a reminder of the impact of integrating lessons into our daily lives and encourages us to continue on our personal growth journey.

Conclusion:

Integrating lessons into daily life is the bridge between knowledge and transformation. It is through consistent practice, reflection, and intentional action that we bring the lessons we learn to life. By embracing a growth mindset, setting actionable goals, creating daily rituals, practicing mindfulness, seeking support, and embracing iteration, we can effectively integrate the valuable lessons into our daily routines. Remember, it is a continuous process, and it requires dedication and perseverance. As we navigate our daily lives, we must remain mindful of the lessons we have learned and actively seek opportunities to apply them.

Integrating lessons into daily life requires conscious effort and a commitment to personal growth. It's important to reflect on the lessons we have learned and identify practical ways to incorporate them into our routines. This may involve making adjustments to our habits, behaviors, or mindset.

Setting actionable goals is crucial for integrating lessons effectively. By breaking down the lessons into specific and measurable objectives, we can create a roadmap for implementation. These goals should be aligned with our values and personal growth aspirations, and they should be realistic and achievable.

Creating daily rituals can support the integration process. By incorporating the lessons into our daily routines, they become ingrained in our habits and become a natural part of our lives. This could involve setting aside dedicated time for reflection, engaging in activities that reinforce the lessons, or practicing gratitude and mindfulness on a regular basis.

Practicing mindfulness is a powerful tool for integrating lessons into daily life. By staying present and aware, we can consciously apply the lessons to our thoughts, actions, and interactions. Mindfulness helps us align our behavior with our intentions and values, ensuring that we consistently live out the lessons we have learned.

Seeking accountability and support can enhance the integration process. Sharing our goals and progress with others who are also committed to personal growth can provide valuable feedback, encouragement, and motivation. It's important to surround ourselves with a supportive community that uplifts and inspires us to stay committed to integrating the lessons into our lives.

Embracing iteration and adaptation is key. As we integrate lessons, we may encounter challenges or discover new insights. It's important to be flexible and willing to adjust our approach as needed. Embracing a mindset of continuous improvement allows us to learn from our experiences, make necessary adjustments, and refine our integration process.

Finally, celebrating progress along the way is essential. Recognizing the positive changes and growth that have resulted from integrating the lessons reinforces our commitment and motivation. It serves as a reminder of the transformative power of personal growth and encourages us to continue integrating new lessons into our lives.

In conclusion, integrating lessons into daily life is a transformative journey. It requires reflection, goal-setting, daily rituals, mindfulness, accountability, adaptation, and celebration. By consciously applying the lessons we have learned, we can cultivate personal growth, enhance our well-being, and create a more fulfilling and purposeful life. Remember, the true value of lessons lies in their application, so embrace the opportunity to integrate them into your daily life and experience the positive changes they can bring.

Chapter 47: Stepping out of comfort zones and embracing challenges.

Introduction:

In life, it's easy to get comfortable with what we know and what feels familiar. We tend to stick to our routines, avoid risks, and shy away from the unknown. However, true personal growth and development happen when we step out of our comfort zones and embrace challenges. This chapter explores the importance of stretching ourselves beyond our limits, the benefits of embracing discomfort, and practical strategies for expanding our comfort zones.

The comfort zone and its limitations:

The comfort zone refers to the familiar and predictable state where we feel safe and at ease. While it provides a sense of security, it can also hinder our growth and limit our potential. Remaining in our comfort zones restricts us from experiencing new opportunities, acquiring new skills, and discovering our true capabilities. Stepping out of our comfort zones is essential for personal growth, as it allows us to overcome fears, expand our skills, and develop resilience.

Embracing discomfort:

Stepping out of our comfort zones means willingly exposing ourselves to discomfort and uncertainty. It involves facing challenges that may initially make us feel anxious or afraid. However, it's important to remember that discomfort is often a sign of growth. By embracing discomfort, we open ourselves up to new experiences, learning opportunities, and personal breakthroughs. It's through challenging ourselves that we discover our strengths, build resilience, and develop a growth mindset.

Benefits of stepping out of comfort zones:

Stepping out of our comfort zones offers numerous benefits that contribute to our personal and professional development. It helps us expand our horizons, broaden our perspective, and develop new skills. By embracing challenges, we become more adaptable, creative, and open-minded. Stepping out of our comfort zones also boosts our self-confidence and self-esteem as we overcome obstacles and achieve personal milestones. Additionally, it enhances our problem-solving abilities and builds our capacity to handle change effectively.

Strategies for stepping out of comfort zones:

1.Start with small steps: Begin by taking small, manageable steps outside of your comfort zone. This could involve trying a new activity, speaking up in a meeting, or engaging in a social event. Gradually increase the level of challenge as you become more comfortable with discomfort.

2.Set clear goals: Define specific goals that require you to step out of your comfort zone. Write them down and create an action plan to achieve them. Having clear objectives will provide focus and motivation as you navigate through challenging situations.

3.Adopt a growth mindset: Embrace the belief that challenges and failures are opportunities for growth. Instead of fearing mistakes or setbacks, view them as valuable learning experiences. Emphasize the process of learning and improvement rather than solely focusing on outcomes.

4.Seek support and accountability: Surround yourself with a supportive network of friends, mentors, or coaches who can provide guidance and encouragement as you step outside your comfort zone. Share your goals and progress with them, and lean on them for support during challenging times.

5.Practice self-compassion: Be kind to yourself as you navigate unfamiliar territory. Understand that growth takes time and that setbacks are a natural part of the process. Treat yourself with compassion and celebrate your efforts, regardless of the outcome.

6.Embrace failure as a learning opportunity: Shift your perspective on failure. See it as an opportunity to learn, grow, and refine your approach. By reframing failure as feedback, you'll be more willing to take risks and embrace challenges.

7.Cultivate a growth mindset: Develop a mindset that embraces challenges and views setbacks as opportunities for growth. Believe in your ability to learn, adapt, and improve. Emphasize the journey of personal growth rather than fixating on immediate results.

Conclusion:

Stepping out of our comfort zones and embracing challenges is a powerful catalyst for personal growth and development. It allows us to push our boundaries, discover new strengths, and unlock our full potential. While it may feel uncomfortable and uncertain at times, the rewards of stepping outside our comfort zones are immense.

By embracing discomfort, we open ourselves up to new experiences and opportunities that can shape our lives in profound ways. We develop resilience, adaptability, and problem-solving skills that help us navigate through life's challenges. Each time we face a fear or overcome an obstacle, we gain confidence in our abilities and expand our belief in what we can achieve.

It's important to remember that stepping out of our comfort zones doesn't mean taking reckless risks or throwing ourselves into situations without proper preparation. It's about taking calculated and thoughtful steps towards growth. We can start small, gradually increasing the level of challenge as we build confidence and competence.

The strategies mentioned earlier can guide us in our journey of stepping outside our comfort zones. Setting clear goals, seeking support, and practicing self-compassion are all essential elements of this process. Additionally, adopting a growth mindset and reframing failure as a learning opportunity helps us embrace challenges with a positive and proactive attitude.

As we continue to step outside our comfort zones, we become more adaptable, resilient, and open-minded individuals. We learn to embrace change and uncertainty, knowing that growth lies just beyond our comfort zones. We become better equipped to handle new situations, explore new interests, and seize opportunities that come our way.

It's important to remember that stepping out of our comfort zones is not a one-time event. It's a lifelong journey of continuous growth and self-discovery. As we evolve, our comfort zones expand, and we become more comfortable with discomfort. What once seemed daunting becomes our new norm, and we find ourselves seeking new challenges to fuel our personal growth.

In conclusion, Chapter 47 emphasizes the significance of stepping out of our comfort zones and embracing challenges. It highlights the benefits, strategies, and mindset shifts required to navigate this transformative process. By venturing beyond the familiar, we unlock our true potential, cultivate resilience, and create a life of fulfillment and growth. So, embrace discomfort, challenge your limits, and step boldly into the unknown. Your greatest achievements await you outside your comfort zone.

Chapter 48: Actualizing dreams and goals.

———

Dreams and goals are the fuel that drives us forward in life. They ignite our passions, inspire our actions, and give us a sense of purpose and direction. However, dreams and goals alone are not enough. To turn them into reality, we need to take deliberate and consistent action.

This chapter explores the process of actualizing our dreams and goals, providing practical strategies and insights to help us transform our aspirations into tangible results.

The first step in actualizing our dreams and goals is to clarify what we truly want. We need to define our vision with clarity and specificity. This involves identifying our core values, passions, and aspirations. By understanding what truly matters to us, we can set meaningful goals that align with our authentic selves.

Once we have a clear vision, it's important to break it down into smaller, actionable steps. Setting milestones and creating a roadmap helps us stay focused and motivated along the way. We can create short-term and long-term goals, each contributing to the overall vision.

To increase our chances of success, it's crucial to develop a plan and establish a system of accountability. This involves creating a strategic action plan, outlining the specific tasks and actions required to move closer to our goals. Additionally, we can enlist the support of mentors, coaches, or an accountability partner who can provide guidance and hold us accountable to our commitments.

Another important aspect of actualizing dreams and goals is cultivating a growth mindset. This mindset allows us to view challenges as opportunities for learning and growth. We embrace setbacks as valuable feedback and use them to adjust our strategies and approach. With a growth mindset, we persist in the face of obstacles and remain resilient in pursuit of our dreams.

Taking consistent action is key to turning our dreams into reality. It's important to prioritize our goals and allocate time and resources accordingly. This may involve making sacrifices, developing new habits, and managing our time effectively. By consistently showing up and putting in the effort, we build momentum and inch closer to our desired outcomes.

Throughout the journey of actualizing our dreams and goals, it's essential to maintain a positive mindset and believe in ourselves. Self-belief is a powerful force that fuels our motivation and propels us forward. We need to silence our inner critic, replace self-doubt with self-confidence, and surround ourselves with positive influences and support.

Celebrating progress and acknowledging achievements along the way is also important. Recognizing our efforts and milestones boosts our motivation and reinforces our belief in our ability to achieve our dreams. It's important to cultivate gratitude and practice self-reflection, appreciating how far we've come and the lessons we've learned.

Lastly, flexibility and adaptability are crucial when actualizing dreams and goals. Life is unpredictable, and circumstances may change along the way. We need to be willing to adjust our plans and strategies as necessary while keeping our vision intact. Being open to new opportunities and embracing change allows us to navigate obstacles and stay on course.

In conclusion, actualizing dreams and goals is a transformative process that requires clarity, action, resilience, and belief in oneself. By defining our vision, setting achievable goals, taking consistent action, and maintaining a growth mindset, we can turn our dreams into reality. With determination and perseverance, we can create a life that aligns with our deepest aspirations and experience the fulfillment that comes from actualizing our dreams.

Chapter 49: Inspiring and motivating others.

———

Inspiring and motivating others is a powerful skill that can have a profound impact on individuals and teams. When we inspire and motivate others, we empower them to reach their full potential, achieve their goals, and contribute their best to the world. In this chapter, we will explore strategies and techniques for effectively inspiring and motivating others.

The first step in inspiring and motivating others is to lead by example. Our own actions, attitude, and enthusiasm serve as a powerful source of inspiration. When we demonstrate passion, dedication, and a positive mindset, we inspire others to do the same. By modeling the behavior and values we want to see in others, we create a ripple effect that encourages others to step up and take action.

Another important aspect of inspiring and motivating others is to understand their individual needs and aspirations. Everyone is motivated by different things, and it's essential to tailor our approach accordingly. We can take the time to get to know the individuals we are working with, understand their strengths, interests, and goals, and find ways to align their passions with the tasks or projects at hand. By tapping into their intrinsic motivations, we can ignite a sense of purpose and enthusiasm.

Communication plays a vital role in inspiring and motivating others. We need to effectively communicate our vision, goals, and expectations to ensure clarity and alignment. By painting a compelling picture of the future and articulating the value and impact of their contributions, we can inspire others to go the extra mile. It's important to listen actively, show empathy, and provide constructive feedback to foster a supportive and collaborative environment.

Recognition and appreciation are powerful motivators. Acknowledging and celebrating the achievements and efforts of others boosts their confidence and motivation. Taking the time to express genuine gratitude and providing positive feedback creates a positive and encouraging atmosphere. Additionally, creating opportunities for growth and development, such as offering training or mentorship programs, shows our investment in their personal and professional advancement.

Inspiring and motivating others also involves creating a culture of trust and empowerment. When individuals feel trusted and empowered, they are more likely to take ownership of their work, explore innovative solutions, and take calculated risks. Providing autonomy and fostering a safe space for creativity and experimentation allows individuals to unleash their full potential and contribute their unique perspectives and ideas.

Setting clear goals and expectations is crucial for motivating others. By establishing SMART (Specific, Measurable, Achievable, Relevant, Time-bound) goals, we provide a clear roadmap and direction. Regularly reviewing progress, providing support and guidance, and celebrating milestones help individuals stay focused and motivated. It's important to provide regular feedback and course corrections to ensure continuous growth and improvement.

Leadership plays a pivotal role in inspiring and motivating others. A great leader inspires trust, leads with integrity, and fosters a positive and inclusive culture. By being approachable, supportive, and encouraging, leaders create an environment where individuals feel valued and motivated to give their best. Effective leaders also delegate responsibilities and empower others to take on leadership roles, fostering a sense of ownership and accountability.

Lastly, storytelling can be a powerful tool for inspiring and motivating others. Sharing personal anecdotes, success stories, and lessons learned creates an emotional connection and inspires individuals to overcome challenges and persevere. By highlighting the impact of their work and the positive difference they can make, we inspire a sense of purpose and ignite their motivation to contribute.

In conclusion, inspiring and motivating others is a skill that can transform individuals and teams. By leading by example, understanding individual motivations, effective communication, recognition, creating a culture of trust and empowerment, setting clear goals, and providing leadership, we can inspire and motivate others to reach their full potential. When we inspire and motivate others, we create a positive and empowering environment that fosters growth, collaboration, and success for all

Chapter 50: The ongoing path to becoming the hero of your own life.

———

Becoming the hero of your own life is a journey that never truly ends. It's a continuous process of growth, self-discovery, and transformation. In this final chapter, we will explore the ongoing path to becoming the hero of your own life and living a fulfilling and purposeful existence.

1.Embrace the hero's mindset: The hero's mindset is characterized by courage, resilience, and a commitment to personal growth. Embrace the belief that you have the power to shape your destiny and overcome any obstacles that come your way. Develop a positive attitude and view challenges as opportunities for growth and learning.

2.Set meaningful goals: Continuously set meaningful and challenging goals that align with your values and aspirations. These goals serve as guiding stars, giving you direction and purpose. Break them down into actionable steps and celebrate your progress along the way. Regularly revisit and revise your goals as you evolve and grow.

3.Cultivate self-compassion: Treat yourself with kindness and compassion. Embrace self-care practices that nurture your physical, mental, and emotional well-being. Practice self-acceptance and forgive yourself for past mistakes or failures. Remember that self-compassion is essential for maintaining resilience and staying motivated on your journey.

4.Cultivate relationships: Surround yourself with positive and supportive relationships. Build meaningful connections with people who uplift and inspire you. Nurture these relationships through open communication, empathy, and shared experiences. Collaborate with others, celebrate their successes, and provide support when needed. Remember that we are stronger together.

5.Continuously learn and grow: Commit to lifelong learning and personal development. Engage in activities that expand your knowledge, skills, and perspectives. Read books, attend workshops, take courses, and seek out new experiences. Embrace a growth mindset that embraces curiosity and a willingness to learn from both successes and failures.

6.Practice gratitude: Cultivate a mindset of gratitude and appreciation. Regularly reflect on the blessings and positive aspects of your life. Express gratitude to others and yourself. Gratitude helps shift your focus to the present moment and cultivates a sense of abundance and fulfillment.

7.Give back: Find ways to give back to your community and make a positive impact. Volunteer your time and skills to causes that resonate with your values. Practice acts of kindness and generosity. By contributing to the well-being of others, you create a ripple effect of positivity and inspire others to do the same.

8.Embrace adaptability: Life is full of unexpected twists and turns. Embrace adaptability and embrace change as an opportunity for growth. Be open to new possibilities and be willing to adjust your plans and mindset when necessary.

Cultivate resilience and find strength in your ability to navigate through life's challenges.

9.Celebrate milestones: Take time to celebrate your achievements and milestones along the way. Reflect on how far you have come and acknowledge the progress you have made. Celebrating your successes reinforces a positive self-image and motivates you to continue striving for greatness.

10.Practice self-reflection: Regularly engage in self-reflection to gain insights into your thoughts, emotions, and behaviors. Create space for introspection and examine your values, beliefs, and motivations. Self-reflection allows you to make conscious choices and course corrections, ensuring that you stay aligned with your true self.

Remember that becoming the hero of your own life is not about achieving perfection. It's about embracing your unique journey, accepting yourself fully, and living in alignment with your values and aspirations. Embrace the challenges, setbacks, and triumphs along the way, for they are all part of your growth and transformation. Embrace the ongoing path to becoming the hero of your own life and find fulfillment in the process.

11.Embrace self-discovery: The journey to becoming the hero of your own life involves self-discovery. Take the time to explore your passions, interests, and strengths. Reflect on what brings you joy and fulfillment. Discovering your authentic self allows you to make choices that align with your true desires and values.

12.Practice self-confidence: Cultivate self-confidence and belief in your abilities. Recognize your unique talents and skills, and trust yourself to navigate through challenges. Celebrate your accomplishments and remind yourself of past successes to boost your confidence. Embrace a positive self-image and embrace the belief that you are capable of achieving greatness.

13.Embrace resilience: Life is filled with ups and downs, and resilience is the key to overcoming obstacles. Develop the ability to bounce back from setbacks and adapt to adversity. Cultivate a mindset that views challenges as opportunities for growth. Learn from failures and use them as stepping stones to success. Remember, resilience is not about avoiding challenges but about your ability to rise above them.

14.Seek meaning and purpose: Find meaning and purpose in your life by aligning your actions with your values. Identify what truly matters to you and make choices that reflect those priorities. Engage in activities that bring you joy and fulfillment. When your actions are guided by purpose, you will find a deeper sense of fulfillment and satisfaction.

15.Practice mindfulness: Incorporate mindfulness into your daily life. Be present in the moment and cultivate awareness of your thoughts, emotions, and surroundings. Mindfulness allows you to fully engage with your experiences and make conscious choices. It helps you find balance, reduce stress, and appreciate the beauty of each moment.

16.Seek inspiration: Surround yourself with sources of inspiration. Seek out role models who embody the qualities and values you admire. Read books, listen to podcasts, and engage with content that uplifts and motivates you. Attend workshops or conferences that fuel your passion and expose you to new ideas. Seek inspiration from various sources to keep your journey exciting and dynamic.

17.Embrace personal responsibility: Take ownership of your life and choices. Recognize that you have the power to shape your destiny. Avoid blaming external circumstances or other people for your challenges. Instead, focus on what you can control and take proactive steps to create the life you desire. Embracing personal responsibility empowers you to take charge of your own happiness and success.

18.Practice self-care: Prioritize self-care to nourish your mind, body, and soul. Engage in activities that promote physical well-being, such as regular exercise, healthy eating, and sufficient sleep. Take time for relaxation and rejuvenation. Engage in hobbies or activities that bring you joy and help you recharge. Remember, taking care of yourself is not selfish but essential for your overall well-being.

19.Embrace continuous growth: The path to becoming the hero of your own life is never-ending. Embrace the concept of continuous growth and lifelong learning. Stay curious and open-minded. Seek out opportunities for personal and professional development. Embrace challenges as opportunities for growth and embrace a growth mindset that fosters resilience and adaptability.

20.Share your story: Your journey to becoming the hero of your own life can inspire others. Share your story, struggles, and triumphs with others. By opening up and being vulnerable, you create a connection with others and show them that they are not alone in their own journeys. Your experiences can provide guidance and motivation to those who may be facing similar challenges.

In conclusion, becoming the hero of your own life is a lifelong journey filled with self-discovery, growth, and transformation. Embrace the hero's mindset, set meaningful goals, cultivate self-compassion, and surround yourself with positive relationships

Ending:

As we reach the end of this book, we have explored the many facets of personal growth, resilience, and living a purposeful life. We have delved into the importance of lifelong learning, self-discipline, overcoming procrastination, and integrating new habits. We have discussed the significance of embracing failure and defeat, cultivating resilient thinking, and bouncing back from setbacks and disappointments. We have explored the power of gratitude, mindfulness, and integrating lessons into daily life. We have discussed the importance of stepping out of comfort zones, embracing challenges, and actualizing dreams and goals. We have explored the art of inspiring and motivating others, achieving work-life balance, nurturing relationships, and practicing self-compassion.

Through each chapter, we have uncovered valuable insights, strategies, and techniques to empower ourselves and create a life filled with purpose, fulfillment, and success. We have learned that personal growth is a continuous journey that requires dedication, perseverance, and self-reflection. It is a journey that requires us to become the heroes of our own lives.

As we close this book, it is important to remember that the wisdom and knowledge gained from these pages are merely tools and guidance. It is up to each individual to take these concepts and apply them to their unique circumstances and aspirations. The true power lies in the action we take and the choices we make on a daily basis.

You, the reader, have the ability to shape your destiny, overcome obstacles, and live a life that aligns with your values and passions. It is through consistent effort, self-belief, and a willingness to step out of your comfort zone that you will continue on the path of personal growth and transformation.

Embracing the ongoing journey to become the hero of your own life requires courage, resilience, and a commitment to self-discovery. It involves setting meaningful goals, cultivating positive attitudes, and nurturing relationships. It involves practicing gratitude, mindfulness, and self-compassion. It involves continuously learning, adapting, and embracing new challenges. It involves finding your purpose, embracing your passions, and inspiring others along the way.

As you navigate this ongoing journey, remember that it is not about achieving perfection or reaching a final destination. It is about embracing the process, learning from both successes and failures, and continuously evolving into the best version of yourself.

There will be times when you stumble, face setbacks, or doubt yourself. But remember that these moments are opportunities for growth and self-discovery. Embrace them with resilience, determination, and a belief in your own abilities. Allow yourself to learn from your mistakes, celebrate your victories, and keep moving forward.

In the end, becoming the hero of your own life is a choice—a choice to take control, to live with intention, and to create a life that reflects your truest self. It is a choice to live a life of purpose, passion, and authenticity.

So, as you close this book, take a moment to reflect on the lessons you have learned, the insights you have gained, and the transformations you have experienced. And with renewed determination, step forward into the world as the hero of your own life, ready to embrace the challenges, celebrate the victories, and create a life that is truly extraordinary.

Remember, the power lies within you. It is time to unleash it and embark on this remarkable journey. You have the potential to create a life that is meaningful, purposeful, and fulfilling. Embrace the path to becoming the hero of your own life and let your light shine brightly for the world to see.

May this book serve as a guide, a source of inspiration, and a reminder that you have the power to shape your destiny. May it accompany you on your ongoing journey of growth, transformation, and personal empowerment.

Now, go forth, my fellow hero, and make your mark on the world. Embrace the challenges that come your way and see them as opportunities for growth and self-discovery. Remember that every setback is a chance to learn, to adapt, and to become even stronger.

As you continue on your path to becoming the hero of your own life, keep in mind the lessons you have learned throughout this book. Draw upon the wisdom of stepping out of your comfort zone, embracing challenges, and pursuing your dreams and goals. Inspire and motivate others along the way, for their success and happiness will only further ignite your own.

But also remember to take care of yourself. Practice self-compassion, self-care, and self-reflection. Nurture your well-being, both physical and mental, as you navigate the twists and turns of your journey. Surround yourself with positive relationships, lean on the support of loved ones, and be open to collaboration and connection.

Along this ongoing path, stay curious and never stop learning. Seek knowledge, new experiences, and different perspectives. Embrace the joy of discovery and the excitement of continuous growth. Let your thirst for knowledge propel you forward and keep your mind open to the possibilities that lie ahead.

Celebrate your achievements, no matter how small they may seem. Each step forward is a victory in itself. Take the time to acknowledge your progress, to reflect on how far you have come, and to express gratitude for the lessons learned along the way. Celebrate not only your successes but also the resilience and determination that have brought you to this point.

And as you become more aware of your own power and potential, remember the importance of giving back. Use your skills, talents, and resources to make a positive impact in the lives of others. Extend a helping hand, lend an ear, or support a cause close to your heart. By uplifting those around you, you contribute to a better world for all.

As we part ways, know that the journey to becoming the hero of your own life does not end here. It is a lifelong endeavor, an ongoing commitment to personal growth and self-improvement. The road may have twists and turns, and there will be moments of doubt and uncertainty. But have faith in yourself and in your ability to overcome any obstacles that come your way.

You are the hero of your own life, and this is your story to write. Embrace each chapter, for they are the building blocks of your personal narrative. Trust in your own strength, resilience, and determination. Believe in the extraordinary potential that lies within you.

So, go forth with courage, my friend. Embrace the ongoing path to becoming the hero of your own life. Let your actions be guided by your values, your dreams, and your passion. And as you continue to grow, inspire others to embark on their own journeys of self-discovery and personal empowerment.

Remember, the power to create a life of purpose, fulfillment, and happiness resides within you. Embrace it, nurture it, and let it shine brightly. You have all that you need to become the hero of your own life. Now, go and make your story a legend worth telling.

Ingram Content Group UK Ltd.
Milton Keynes UK
UKHW020638260723
425809UK00015B/538

9 798223 144380